SOCIAL
RESEARCH
and
SOCIAL
POLICY

PRENTICE-HALL SERIES IN SOCIAL POLICY
Howard E. Freeman, Editor

Howard E. Freeman
Clarence C. Sherwood

SOCIAL RESEARCH and SOCIAL POLICY

prentice-hall, inc.
englewood cliffs, new jersey

Library of Congress Catalog Card No.: 77-107960

Current printing (last digit)

10   9   8   7   6   5   4   3   2   1

Printed in the United States of America

PRENTICE-HALL INTERNATIONAL, INC., London
PRENTICE-HALL OF AUSTRALIA, PTY. LTD., Sydney
PRENTICE-HALL OF CANADA, LTD., Toronto
PRENTICE-HALL OF INDIA PRIVATE LIMITED, New Delhi
PRENTICE-HALL OF JAPAN, INC., Tokyo

PREFACE

Some readers of this volume may be disappointed that the methodological procedures discussed are not fully explicated; others that there are some matters discussed in technical terms. We have tried to write the book so that it would be useful to a broad audience, and be of interest to both graduate and undergraduate students in the social sciences and in various professional schools, as well as to researchers and practitioners in the health, education and welfare fields.

The level of the book is an effort to balance the interests and technical training that varies so greatly within this broad audience. It should be emphasized that *Social Research and Social Policy* is not a substitute for the several excellent general methodology texts that are available. The references contain citations to them as well as to some of the advanced material that elaborates technical procedures.

Finally, it should be noted, our intent to place the research processes in the context of the social policy arena has required us to oversimplify the way the world of policy development and social action operates. Perhaps it is fairer to say that we have found it necessary to view policy-making and program implementation in terms of how it should operate rather than how it often does. Hopefully, the volume will be a modest contribution to the more systematic and rational development of the social policy and social action environment.

Mary Elizabeth Hintze undertook much of the library work connected with writing this volume. Lillian Oates and Kathleen McConnell undertook the various chores involved in preparation of the manuscript. We are most grateful for their participation.

A few short months before his untimely death, Edward A. Suchman reviewed the volume. His comments and constructive criticisms proved most valuable.

HOWARD E. FREEMAN

Brandeis University
and
Russell Sage Foundation

CLARENCE C. SHERWOOD

John Jay College of the City University of New York

CONTENTS

vii

Chapter 1

THE SOCIAL-POLICY PERSPECTIVE

The view of the authors of this book is that the social scientist should direct his work toward the solution of contemporary social problems and that the amelioration of the ills of our society should be a guiding force in the work of social researchers. This position is a controversial one. (For an excellent discussion of the controversy, see Kelman, 1968). Many social scientists hold that the primary goal of social science is the discovery and verification of principles of social behavior, whether or not they are immediately useful in programs to improve social life and social conditions. The reader is, of course, free to choose between these perspectives. But the simple fact is that considerable research activity and the work of many social researchers is, whether by desire or circumstance, intertwined with efforts to identify, understand, and temper the social ills of our communities. (See Lerner, 1959, and the articles in Lazarsfeld, Sewell, and Wilensky, 1967).

The purpose of this book is to provide an understanding of how social research can contribute to social policy. More specifically, its aims are threefold: first, to describe what the social policy researcher does; second, to indicate some of the more important and useful perspectives, skills, and techniques of social-policy research; and, third, to inform the reader of some of the major pitfalls and problems which occur when the social scientist elects a social-policy orientation.

Social scientists contribute to the reduction of the problems of community life in a variety of ways. Some participate in the affairs of their communities as responsible citizens. Others actually work full, or more often part-time, on the "firing line," directing or sharing responsibility for social action and rehabilitation programs. Still others engage themselves in what is believed here to be the most important and strategic role of all, the development and implementation of social policy. (National Academy of Sciences, 1969).

Since social-policy research cannot be discussed profitably in any depth without first considering social policy itself, an examination of the nature of social policy will precede our treatment of social-policy research, the central concern of this book. At the outset, however, it may be useful to offer a preliminary definition of social-policy research. *Social-policy research refers to the use of the methods and findings of social research in the development and carrying out of communal efforts to improve the social and physical environments of the members of the community and to better their psychological and physical lives.*

Social-policy research generally is no different from other types of social and psychological investigations, either in terms of the empirical perspective of the researcher or the research principles and techniques which guide him. It is in the selection of the problems and the goals of the research that social-policy research is distinguished from so-called "pure" research. The social-policy researcher sees himself within a context of social problems, social action, and social change. The way he selects and formulates his research problems, as well as his aspirations for the utilization of his work, are influenced accordingly. Thus, social-policy research can be thought of as the application of general social-research methods, under a particular set of circumstances and toward certain specified ends, by individuals with training in the social sciences and an orientation toward the solution of social problems (Brayfield, 1967; Marrow, 1964).

What Is Social Policy?

Social policy is a lay term, not a technical one, and like most such terms, it defies simple definition. (See, for example, the articles in Ranney, 1968, and Bauer and Gergen, 1968). At least four different uses or definitions can be distinguished, however:

> *1. Social policy as a philosophical concept.* In an abstract sense, social policy is the principle whereby the members of large organizations and political entities collectively seek enduring solutions to the problems that affect them—almost the opposite, that is, of rugged individualism.

2. *Social policy as a product.* Viewed as a product, social policy consists of the conclusions reached by persons concerned with the betterment of community conditions and social life, and with the amelioration of deviance and social disorganization. Often the product is a document—what the British call a "white paper"—which lays out the intended policy for an organization or political unit.

3. *Social policy as a process.* Here, social policy is the fundamental process by which enduring organizations maintain an element of stability and at the same time seek to improve conditions for their members. Existing social policies are usually never fully developed; they are continually modified in the face of changing conditions and values.

4. *Social policy as a framework for action.* As a framework for action, social policy is both product and process. It assumes the availability of a well-delineated policy which is to be implemented within the context of potential changes in the values, structure, and conditions of the group affected.

The variety of uses and the illusive nature of the concept of social policy play havoc with efforts to describe systematically the components of policy making. The observations that follow, therefore, are at best tentative and speculative.

Some Observations on the Development of Social Policy

Although we currently have only a vague understanding of social-policy development, several basic tasks are usually undertaken by the policy maker. These will be referred to as *planning, program development and implementation,* and *evaluation.* Each of these tasks includes a number of different components including some which require extended discussion.

PLANNING

The planning process includes the identification of the goals of the organization, the assessment of the extent to which actual conditions deviate from those goals, and the development of a general framework or strategy for achieving convergence between goals and existing conditions or behavior. Planning is usually predicated on a desire to reduce the gap between the goal and the reality. In some instances, however, the objective may be to maintain the *status quo* in the face of anticipated deterioration.

The planning process should produce a scheme for accomplishing a convergence between goals and existing conditions, a schedule for doing so, the designation of individuals responsible for carrying out the activities, and the specification of the required human and financial resources.

Setting Goals. Social policy can be developed only in relation to a communal goal or objective (Lecht, 1966). *Goals, from the standpoint of social policy, are standards which have not been fully attained.* Goal setting, in the development of social policy, requires a statement of the desired outcome, which also specifies the condition to be dealt with and establishes a criterion of success. The achievement of an *absolute goal* requires that either an undesirable condition be eliminated or that a desirable one be attained for everyone. *Relative goals* establish standards of achievement in terms of some proportionate improvement of the conditions that exist at some point in time.

What are some examples of goals? One goal in the health area might be the immunization of the entire population against illnesses such as poliomyelitis or whooping cough. This is an absolute goal. The reduction of gonorrhea by 50 per cent would be a relative goal. In education, an absolute goal which has been advocated is the elimination of illiteracy for all persons under 30.

As can be seen from these examples, the setting of social policy requires either assumptions or knowledge about two fundamental aspects of the social situation: values, and existing conditions. The immunization goal at least assumes certain basic societal values concerning health and the minimization of death rates, and perhaps the higher priority of the young over the old. The elimination of illiteracy assumes certain basic societal values concerning education and the importance of literacy to productive participation in our economic system and our democracy. And both these goals, like any relative goal, are based upon the assumption or knowledge that there is room for improvement—that is, that there is a discrepancy between the actual conditions and those specified by the goals.

Assessing Existing Conditions. The need for the policy maker to take existing conditions into account has already been referred to in the discussion of goal setting. In many cases, a knowledge of these conditions exists before the goals are set; information may, in fact, initiate the setting of goals and policy. In any event, an assessment of the empirical situation is required somewhere in the planning process. At one extreme, this assessment may be entirely impressionistic, reflecting only the policy maker's view. At the other extreme, it may result from a systematic research enquiry by technically qualified investigators. If, on the one hand, policy makers believe there is enough agreement among prevailing impressions, they may omit a search for the facts; if, on the other hand, they have reasonably definitive information at hand, they may not take impressions into account at all. Generally, however, their assessment of existing conditions is more likely to be a conglomeration of facts and impressions.

Once estimates of conditions have been obtained, goals may have to be modified. For example, the policy maker may start out with the goal of eliminating all cigarette smoking. But subsequent knowledge of the persistence of smoking may induce him to change his goal to the reduction of cigarette smoking by some specified amount. In some instances, the imperative character of certain goals may motivate the policy maker to obtain more precise estimates or an assessment in greater depth. For example, the objective of eliminating illiteracy may be regarded as so important that the policy maker may insist upon a nationwide testing program, rather than rely on available information on number of years of schooling.

Development of a Strategy. Policy makers naturally should not spend their time developing the details of a social policy unless there is some real possibility of social action. Planning must, therefore, include a notion about how to gain acceptance of the goal and secure a mandate for proceeding toward its achievement. The planning process should also include some ideas about potentially successful means of moving in the desired direction. It is unlikely that a planner will devote much time to a policy if there are no techniques available for handling the problem to which that policy is directed. Similarly, no great effort is likely to be made if the policy maker is going to be completely thwarted in developing and carrying out a program.

Although there is considerable disagreement about the styles which should be employed, planners usually spend a great deal of their time seeking support and legitimization. Some planners maintain that the planning process must begin with legitimization. According to this point of view, based upon an enduring tradition referred to in the social-work field as "self-determinism," one should only develop goals pertaining to matters about which the parties involved have manifested concern; moreover, the goals should constitute an expression of the views of the group or community members involved. Other planners, adopting a similar strategy for different reasons, insist that "indigenously centered" planning, in which the parties affected have a strong role, is the most promising approach, on the grounds that it is essential to success that all such parties be fully involved. Yet others argue for what they refer to as "centrally directed" planning, on the grounds of its greater efficiency and effectiveness. (See Morris and Binstock, 1966, for an extended discussion of planning strategies.) In terms of what happens in actual planning in the real world, the two last types noted, (centrally directed and indigenous planning) may be thought of as polar extremes. About all that should probably be added here about this very complex subject is that the strategy of legitimization is likely to be a crucial part of any planning process.

PROGRAM DEVELOPMENT

Program development refers to the design of specific interventions and ameliorative activities based on the information, analyses, decisions, and recommendations produced in the planning phase. Practicality and feasibility are important considerations in the transition from the broader, more general, value-oriented planning stage to the more detailed, reality-and-action-oriented process of program development. A complete and comprehensive translation of policy goals into program specifications leaves a minimum of decisions for the individuals given the responsibility for the practical operations.

Policy and Practice. Theoretically, the operator or practitioner is an administrator, a supervisor, and a technician. He is responsible for the conduct of the desired intervention in accordance with the specifications of the program design. The policy maker, in developing the program, formulates the principles which define the role of the practitioner, and is responsible for seeing that the program is conducted by the practitioner in accordance with the program specifications.

In practice, however, the responsibility for program development is often vaguely defined, and the program itself is unsystematically shaped. Much of the work of the practitioner in the fields of health, education, and welfare is undertaken on a highly individualized, *ad hoc* basis. General directives are issued and individuals are charged with the responsibility for carrying them out, but considerable discretion, by design or default, may be left to the practitioner. Because of the ambiguities surrounding the carrying out of programs, individuals who are formally or primarily operators take on policy-making functions as well.

An illustration might be useful here. In a university, for example, both policy and procedures have to be developed for the admission of students. The board of trustees and the president may authorize the dean and a committee of the faculty to develop admission criteria. On the one hand, that committee may draw up detailed specifications of all the criteria to be taken into consideration: College Board scores, standing in class, extracurricular activities, and the like. It may even designate the weight to be given to each of these measures. If the criteria are completely specified, the job of the director of admissions is merely to carry out the directives —obtain the required information, devise scoring schemes, and develop procedures for notifying students of acceptance or rejection. On the other hand, the dean and his committee might report out a vague profile of the types of students they want in the university, and instruct the director of admissions to develop the criteria and the procedures for using them in the selection of students. In the first instance, the dean and the committee have assumed the responsibility for virtually all of the policy formulation and for a considerable portion of the program development; in the second, the responsibility for the program's development has been left entirely to the director of admissions.

Even if the dean and the faculty committee have spelled out all the criteria, however, the day-to-day processing will require some policy decisions of the director of admissions: for example, he may have to evaluate transcripts from foreign schools which use a different grading system. In practice, most high-level administrators engage to some extent in policy making.

It should be obvious that, in the fields of health, education and welfare, at least, the distinctions between operator and policy maker are not likely to be precise—and perhaps cannot and should not be. In the first place, distinctions between procedures and policies are often obscure. Moreover, many individuals shift from policy maker to practitioner and back again. Only the most general policies may be set for the warden of a prison, for example, and he is likely to play a significant policy-making role in setting the goals and general framework for the rehabilitation and care of prisoners. However, he does not order an execution. In this instance, he follows as precisely as possible the mandate of the courts.

The blurred lines in policy formulation, between developing a program and carrying it out, are likely to be particularly evident at the level of major federal agencies. Commissioners of such agencies as the Social Security Administration and the Food and Drug Administration are charged with heavy day-to-day administrative duties. Their primary role is to carry out the policies and programs formulated by the policy makers, Congress and the Departmental Secretaries. However, Congress rarely outlines, in its legislation, specifically how matters must be handled, and the directives of the secretaries are not necessarily much more detailed. Furthermore, the Secretaries of the Departments may believe that the Commissioners are best qualified to draw up the precise programs. Thus, the Commissioners will have important program development functions to carry out, which in turn are likely to involve numerous, or at least subtle aspects of policy.

While the distinction between policy making and practice is far from clear, there are two critical tasks that must always be accomplished as part of program development and implementation. These are the development of an impact model and the selection of a target population.

The development of an impact model. An impact model is an attempt to translate theoretical notions regarding the regulation, modification, and control of social behavior or community conditions into hypotheses on which an action can be based. It may be helpful to distinguish between what might be called implicit and explicit impact models. Fully explicit models are rare. Too often, impact models consist of nothing more than the implicit assumptions which underly the program's operation. These assumptions may have been drawn from previous studies, undertaken on small samples or in other locales—or they may have little or no empirical base at all, being drawn from the untested ways in which practitioners have performed in the past.

The absence of an explicitly stated impact model prevents replication of the program and severely limits the opportunities for controlling its quality and evaluating its effectiveness. If the parties involved in program development and implementation fail (or refuse) to apply themselves to unraveling and specifying the assumptions and principles underlying the program, there is no basis for understanding what they are doing, why they are doing it, or even for judging whether or not they are doing what they intend to do (Freeman and Sherwood, 1965). Even if their program is capable of achieving the objectives set for it—an assumption seldom based on any evidence, by the way—without an explicit impact model there is no basis for understanding why it worked or for reproducing it and its effects on a broader scale and in other communities.

Impact models, implicit or explicit, are predicated on some notion of cause and effect. But, because of the present state of knowledge in the social and behavioral sciences, the impact model is rarely based upon a set of principles and generalizations which are grounded in definite evidence. More often, it is a vaguely operationalized hypothesis about cause and effect. A fully developed social policy should try, during the evaluation stage, to examine empirically the cogency of the hypothesized causal explanation.

The impact model must include a statement concerning the stimulus or input, an hypothesis about what changes the input will produce, and a theory or proposition about how that change will affect the behavior or condition the policy maker is seeking to modify. For example, the policy maker may have decided that there is insufficient utilization of mental-health services by undereducated individuals. The goal of his program is a substantial increase in such use. The policy maker may develop a program of education about mental health as the means of accomplishing the goal. Even if the program does not explicitly say so, he is presuming that an educational program (the stimulus or input) causes changes in people's views or attitudes. Further, he is assuming that *his* program will produce changes in attitudes, and that the changes in attitudes will lead to greater utilization of mental-health services. Finally, he is probably positing that a greater utilization of such services will improve mental health. Embedded in his chain of thought is the assumption that individuals who use psychiatric services have attitudes which differ from those who avoid treatment.

The impact model consists, then, of a minimum of three hypotheses: The first hypothesis, in this case, is a simple one, i.e., that a program of mental-health education will change attitudes; the second hypothesis is that changes in attitudes produce changes in behavior; and the third is that the experimentally changed attitudes are in the same relationship to the behavior in question as attitudes which exist under "natural" conditions. Further development of the impact model would require both the identification of the specific set of attitudes which are related to the utilization of mental-health services and the theoretical derivation of the specific procedures by which those attitudes can be changed. The derived hypothesis is that only persons who change in specified ways will become more likely to use the services.[1]

Consider another example. A remedial reading program is proposed as a means of curtailing delinquent behavior. The first hypothesis may be that a remedial reading program will improve the reading of the program's recipients. The second hypothesis is that reading performance is related to delinquent behavior, i.e., the better the reading the less the likelihood of delinquency. The third hypothesis is that the experimentally changed reading performances are in the same relationship to delinquency as in natural conditions. The further development of the impact model requires both the identification of the specific aspects of reading performance which are related to delinquency and the theoretical derivation of the specific procedures by which reading can be improved. The derived hypothesis is that those whose reading improves will thereby become less likely to commit delinquent acts. The development of impact models and the utility of research in doing so is discussed in detail in Chapter 4.

Selection of the Target Population. The selection of the target population is the second important aspect of program development and effectuation. *"Target population" is shorthand for the group for which the program is designed and which it is hoped will be helped by the program.* In most instances, decisions about program development require an understanding of the needs of various aggregates within the community. Ordinarily, the first step toward the identification of the target population takes place during the planning phase. At that time, a case is made for the existence of groups whose behavior or standard of living diverges from a desired state. During the program's development, the client or recipient population must be carefully specified. For example, if the reduction of illiteracy among persons of a certain age is the selected

---

[1] The question, "More likely than whom?" is actually a rather complicated one. It is not enough that the intervention lead to a greater use of the services in the future unless there are sound reasons for assuming that no increase would have taken place without the intervention. The derived hypothesis, therefore, is that persons who change in specified ways will be more likely to use the services, subsequent to their participation in the intervention, than they would have if they had not changed in the specified ways.

goal, preliminary information must be obtained about the number, characteristics, and residential location of illiterates in the community. General decisions about the nature, scope, and geographical location of the program can then be made.

Criticisms are frequently made in the public arena about the failure of programs to meet the needs of community members, often justifiably. Policy makers may fail to define the target population adequately and consider its characteristics fully.

The selection of target populations is closely associated with the development of an impact model. In theory, the identification of the target population and its characteristics should precede the development of the impact model. In practice, however, it is often impossible to decide on the target population without considering the impact model as well. The usual procedure is to revise the impact model repeatedly on the basis of knowledge of the population and, concurrently, to narrow and re-specify the target population on the basis of tentative decisions about the impact model. The person charged with the development of a program to reduce illiteracy, let us say, plans to use a teaching machine. When he learns that the particular cultural group with the highest rate of illiteracy has great fear of mechanical and electrical devices, he must either modify his impact model or redefine the target population. Eventually, of course, it is necessary to decide firmly on both the impact model and the target population so that the final details can be worked out and the program turned over to the practitioners who will carry it out.

Additional Aspects of Program Development and Implementation. There are many other factors which must be taken into consideration in the development and carrying out of a program. However, they tend to be related specifically to the program being developed. They shall be mentioned here only in passing, although they will come up again in our subsequent discussions of social-policy research.

Usually, it is necessary to specify such matters as the table of organization of the agency that is going to carry out the program; to lay out a budget for the conduct of the program; to indicate how finances, manpower, and other resources are going to be obtained; to coordinate the program with existing services; and to lay the groundwork for its acceptance by key community leaders, relevant professionals, and clients or recipients of the program. Without considering these elements further, we should point out that the initial spadework in these areas is usually undertaken as part of the planning process although specific proposals are rarely fully outlined at that time.

In the beginning stage, the policy maker takes a plan and renders it workable by anticipating or prognosticating the considerations that will be involved at the time it is put into effect. Part of the mystique which surrounds the successful policy maker is related to his ability to develop and activate his program at an opportune time and in an opportune context. He is perhaps like the businessman who starts a sale of winter coats on the day the weather turns cold and who tries not to place his advertisement in the newspaper on the day of an important event. While we hold that social-policy research is an important input into the process of program development, it is not to be denied that the intuition and political savvy of the policy maker are often the key determinants of success or failure.

Administrative procedures and on-the-job practices are other considerations which are directly related to the program being developed. In many instances the policy maker does not need to specify all the elements of the program's development and operation. For example, few policy makers would feel it necessary to specify the particular needle the public-health physician is to use in the treatment of venereal disease. Moreover, the policy maker himself may not possess the technical knowledge necessary for the specification of procedures in his program outline. No Secretary of Health, Education, and Welfare, for example, could be a competent practitioner in all the programs within his domain. However, it is possible that the policy maker may assume more communality of knowhow than actually exists among his practitioners and operators, many of whom have been trained in different and highly specialized fields. In this case, the policy maker must know the level of generalization that is possible, given the special qualifications of his practitioners and operators. The relevance of the explicit specification of administrative procedures and detailed operations will become more apparent in the discussion of evaluation which follows.

EVALUATION

Viewed broadly, and to some extent ideally, evaluation provides the basis for the policy maker's decisions concerning the continuation, modification, expansion, or elimination of programs directed toward the amelioration of social ills. Using evaluation procedures, the policy maker seeks to determine, first, whether or not the program was carried out in accordance with the prescriptions set forth in the planning and development stages and, second, whether or not it worked. Third, within a broader context, he tries to ascertain whether the expenditure of resources has been efficient in comparison with alternative means of achieving the same objective. In practice, the process of evaluation may range from a general, impressionistic appraisal of a program to a carefully designed experiment (Suchman, 1967).

From the standpoint of social policy, provision should be made for the evaluation of at least all newly planned and developed programs. The policy maker's influence is at stake, particularly these days, unless he can produce evidence that the program has actually been conducted according to its specifications. More and more, policy makers are being challenged to demonstrate the impact of programs, to show, that is, that the programs reduce the disparity between goals and existing behavior or conditions. Given the magnitude of many of these programs and the financial and human resources they require, their existence is difficult to justify solely on theoretical or traditional grounds. Pressures for the continued expansion of health, education, and welfare programs has increased the demand for serious evaluations.

For purposes of discussion, evaluation can be said to consist of two activities: assessing how well the program is carried out, and measuring its impact. Both these activities provide the policy maker with opportunities to reassert his participation in the operations of programs.

The Assessment of How Well a Program Is Carried Out. There are at least two important reasons why the execution of a program must be assessed. First, funds are authorized for the conduct of programs with specified characteristics, and there is an administrative, often a legal, obligation to see that the requirements are complied with. Second, a basic component of studies to measure the impact of a program is a known, controlled, and repeatable stimulus or intervention. Clearly, it is not of much value to know whether a program worked unless we also know what it consisted of.

The carrying out of a program is ordinarily assessed through anthropological, or field, investigations. These investigations determine whether the various procedures are being carried out as specified, or at least whether they are derived from the principles explicated in the program's design (Suchman, 1967). It is also important to know whether the program is reaching the target population.

The person without experience in remedial and rehabilitative efforts may not be aware of the tremendous discrepancies that exist between what professionals say should be done and what actually is done. The development of procedures for evaluating the congruence between the plan and the conduct of a program is a difficult task. Part of the problem is that privacy and secrecy surround many operations. The health field is a classic illustration of this phenomenon, but it is true in other fields as well. Professors and teachers object strenuously to the invasion of their classrooms, and so do virtually all other occupational groups who identify themselves as professionals.

The tradition of privacy is not the only impediment to an adequate assessment of performance. A great deal of data must be constantly obtained and analyzed. It is costly, and it requires additional administrative and other personnel who are trained to do the job. Studies of the development of assessments are relatively scarce, but they all point to the need for an extensive commitment on the part of both the policy maker and the practitioner. Even computerized systems add extensively to the workloads and cost of a program (Cline, Freeman, and Wheeler, 1968). Some comments on the specific technical issues involved will be found elsewhere in this book; it is important to note, however, that despite a reawakening interest in what sociologists refer to as "field work," the methodology of observation and of studying ongoing social interactions is underdeveloped (Becker, 1961; Whyte, 1955).

Measuring a Program's Impact. The impact of a program is traditionally confused with estimating whether or not it is being conducted in an appropriate way. Often, if a program is conducted in conformity with certain specified standards, and particularly if qualified professionals are involved, it is claimed that it can be automatically regarded as successful. Success, in this instance, is defined in terms of the quality of the services delivered (Suchman, 1967). It is often believed, by those who rely on the quality of the service rendered, that if a program is run properly it can also be assumed that the desired changes are taking place and that these changes are due to the program.

The judgment of the quality of a program has a place in the evaluation process, of course. It is obviously expedient and rational to test out only programs that have a theoretical basis and that are carefully designed and conducted. But professional judgment cannot substitute for the experimental measurement of impact. Impact can only be assessed through systematic, empirical research, either through the planned, experimental manipulation of events or behavior, or through the systematic observation of natural occurrences. The critical role of experimental design in the assessment of impact may be obvious, and many policy makers and practitioners may intellectually accept their importance, but there has been a general reluctance to abide by experimental principles in the assessment of the worth of social-rehabilitation programs.

In our view, *impact is that difference between pre-program behavior or conditions and post-program behavior or conditions which can legitimately be attributed to the intervention.* Well-run programs or desired change are not enough; the changes must be observable and clearly due to the program—or impact, by our definition, has not occurred. Unfortunately, the experimental evaluation of impact is not a simple matter (we discuss it in detail in Chapter 5). Here we merely make some key points so that the reader can appreciate the general nature of the task.

In its crudest form, an experiment involves the observation and measurement of a particular phenomenon at two points in time, an artificial or natural change having occurred between the two. All of us experiment constantly: this is the way we learn how to get along in our environment. We may go into a restaurant, cut into a steak and taste it, put salt on it and taste it again, and then decide for ourselves whether we are better or worse off. Clinicians often do exactly the same thing. They make an hypothesis about a patient or client, provide a pill or some other type of therapy, and then judge or ask the patient to judge whether or not there has been an improvement in his condition. But as we have stated emphatically, the policy maker concerned with experimental evaluation cannot be satisfied with merely introducing a program and observing the changes that take place. There must be a basis for confidence that the introduced change accounts for the observed difference. Thus, he employs control groups, and contrasts what happens to them in comparison with the persons or objects which constitute the experimental group. In some experiments, the control group receives no treatment, or no exposure to the program. In many evaluation studies, as we shall discuss in Chapter 5, control groups receive typical or ordinary programs rather than no treatment.

There is a well-defined set of procedures for the assignment of subjects to control and experimental groups. With few exceptions, ideal experimental design requires the investigator to use a *randomization procedure, i.e., the assignment of cases to various groups on a chance basis, as in a lottery.* The primary purpose of randomization is to eliminate all other possible determinants of impact or outcome except the experimental stimulus or change. A gourmet who is also a scientist, for example, would not taste one bite of steak, put salt on a second one, and then evaluate the difference. He would cut the steak into equal pieces, give each piece a number, sort them out into two piles on a random basis, salt one pile, distribute all the pieces of both piles randomly in a platter, and then record his reactions to each piece by number. If the salt has made a difference, the numbers he records in the "improved" column should correspond to the numbers of the salted pieces.

While the steak experiment is perhaps not worth the effort every time we eat, the owner of a restaurant chain might undertake some such test, say with beef stew, if he wanted to provide a standard recipe to a number of chefs. He might actually undertake a more elegant experiment, using a panel of judges rather than a single person and varying the quantities of salt so that he would have a series of experimental groups as well as the control one. And this is the way it should be in the health, education, and welfare fields as well. The object of experimental evaluation is to test whether the specified stimulus, input, or innovative condition makes any difference—that is, whether it reduces the disparity between the goal and the actual behavior or condition.

The use of control groups and of randomization, however, creates great antagonism. To some degree the problem is a strange one, an unwillingness to accept in the sphere of human relations a set of procedures which intellectually and experimentally, in the physical and life sciences, have proved their worth. Practitioners and policy makers argue that experimental evaluation is undemocratic, inhuman, and unpolitical, and they are unwilling to deny services to that part of the population which constitutes the control group.

It would be foolish to deny that there are many practical problems in designing experiments with human subjects, particularly evaluation experiments conducted in the community and not in the laboratory. Nevertheless, it is impossible to develop an adequate social policy in any sphere without experimental evaluations—which at best may be less than perfect investigations from the standpoint of rigorous experimental design.

THE RELATIONSHIPS AMONG THE PLANNING, PROGRAM
DEVELOPMENT AND IMPLEMENTATION, AND EVALUATION

In introducing the various aspects of social policy, we have tried to emphasize the overlap between the various tasks and to point out that the separation of planning, program development, and evaluation is to some extent artificial. Obviously, they are interdependent. Sound evaluation cannot take place when the planning and development of the program have not been thorough. In our discussion of program development, we stressed the importance of explicating both an impact model and the characteristics of a target population, for without them we have no means for observing the extent that practice conforms to the expectations of a program's developers. Further, a knowledge of both the target population and the impact model are absolutely necessary if one is going to design an evaluation experiment. The task, in developing an evaluation experiment, is to transform the program plan into an experiment. The various statements which link the program elements together into an impact model become the hypotheses that are tested in the experiment. The inputs or innovative procedures included in the program model represent the stimuli. In the same sense, unless the planning has been adequate, there is little basis for the development of measures or criteria of outcome.

Some Concluding Observations

In this chapter, we have described some of the tasks of the policy maker as he goes about his work. It would be easier to explicate the policy maker's role and activities if the process of policy making were better understood and more standardized. It is not possible to lay out an exact order of the steps which he takes, and then state the points along the way at which the researcher becomes involved. To do so would be to distort reality far beyond the limits desirable in pedagogy; as it is, considerable oversimplification and artificial systemization has been necessary in order to try to present the framework of policy making. There are, of course, more detailed treatments, for example, Kahn's (1969) volume on planning. In any event, policy making is, at present, largely a clinical matter, something which the various parties can only learn by doing, and unavoidably entails an apprenticeship or an internship. In later chapters, some of the tasks of the policy researcher and the ways he goes about his work will be examined, but given the current state of affairs, no amount of discussion can substitute for the experience one needs for a full understanding of the policy-making role.

Chapter 2

THE CONTRIBUTION OF RESEARCH TO SOCIAL POLICY

Research has a significant part to play in each of the steps involved in developing social policy—in planning, program development and implementation, and in evaluation. The social scientist who is oriented toward policy making and who has the requisite technical skills can contribute importantly. In this chapter, the roles played in policy development by social investigators will be examined. In addition, some of their past and present interests will be described briefly. Social-policy research is a complex matter; it includes what researchers do, how they orient themselves to their tasks, and the product of their activities.

The Role of the Research

While in practice the different roles that researchers take are not always sharply delineated from each other, the characteristics of these various roles can be identified. One criterion is the scope of the researcher's involvement in over-all policy development: Does he participate broadly and generally at each level of policy development, or is his role restricted to some specific part of the process?

The base from which the researcher operates is also an important aspect of his role in policy research: Is he a full-time staff member of the policy-making organization, or is he employed by a somewhat more re-

17

motely related organization such as a university? Another important aspect of his role concerns the intent of the researcher: Is his research directed from the start toward the development of a policy, or is the potential applicability of his findings accidental, and incidental to his own research aims? There are at least four distinguishable roles in policy research, which may be described as: comprehensive participation; fragmented participation; external participation; and serendipitous participation.

COMPREHENSIVE PARTICIPATION

In some instances the research process is considered so important to policy development that the organization has a permanent research section. Some programs, including several major ones sponsored by the federal government, are required by legislation to include such a research unit. For example, the comprehensive planning and action grants awarded by the President's Committee on Delinquency and Youth Development included a requirement to this effect.

The researcher who is employed full-time in an action-oriented organization may participate in policy development at all levels. Ideally, he is called upon during all the phases of policy development, to apply his investigative techniques and sensitivity to social relations and social processes and to evaluate and interpret available research findings with respect to the policy matters at issue. Even in this comprehensive role, however, the policy researcher may be more intensively involved in one aspect of policy development than in others. In one organization the research activities may be primarily directed to the planning process. In another, the development and carrying out of programs may absorb the major share of available research energy; in still a third, evaluation may be the principal task.

The place of the research unit within the formal and informal structure of the organization also varies considerably. For example, the head of the research unit of a social planning agency may be an associate director reporting directly to the chief executive and the board of the organization; in these circumstances he may have considerable power and influence on policy development. In another organization, charged with a similar task, in another locale, the research director may be responsible to someone considerably further down in the organizational hierarchy—in which case he may have little opportunity to influence policy directly. Perhaps most important, he may have little or nothing to say about the allocation of research funds or the use to which his findings are put.

The support of even a modest research unit on a permanent basis, with as little as one or two researchers with the skill and experience to

engage comprehensively and intensively in policy research and development, requires a considerable commitment of resources. It is generally
true, therefore, that research units are maintained only by the larger
policy agencies and that, currently, there are relatively few social researchers with a comprehensive role in the development of policy in the
social-action field.

FRAGMENTED PARTICIPATION

Fragmented participation in policy development, the instance in
which the social investigator is called upon to work on only special parts
of the program's development, is much more common. The possible arrangements he may have with the policy agency vary considerably. He
may be appointed for a long period of time, either as part of a permanent
unit within the agency or on a contract basis, or he may be called upon
on an *ad hoc* basis. As an example of the first case, a policy body may
have a unit which evaluates research; members of such units ordinarily
do not participate in planning or in developing and carrying out programs. As an example of the second, a policy agency may employ a
demographer from a local university as a consultant during the planning
process, specifically to obtain a statistical profile of the community.

The steps of the policy-making process are so interrelated that researchers designated to play fragmented roles may overstep their bounds
or find themselves lured into a broader role by others in the policy-
making group. The difficulties which ensue because of the amorphous
boundaries of fragmented roles are thus often considerable. Many of the
available reports on the relationship of the researcher to social-policy
groups deal with problems prevalent when participation is fragmented.

EXTERNAL PARTICIPATION

Many investigators who conduct policy-making research have no
involvement with policy-making bodies. For example, academic investigators are increasingly undertaking research in social problems of a
policy character. These investigators view their work as directly related
to policy development and it is their intention to influence social policies
through their findings. It is common now for the concluding chapter of
research reports to contain sections on social policy. To cite one, Duff
and Hollingshead (1968) undertook a study of the medical care of persons
of differing economic status in a general hospital affiliated with a large
university, and the differences in the handling of rich and poor patients
which they found prompted them to conclude the volume by suggesting
major modifications in hospital policy. Policy makers associated with

medical-care programs and health-care settings who read Duff and Hollingshead's book may be influenced as much by their policy recommendations as they would if the findings came from units within their own organizations.

The external participant in policy investigations departs least from the traditions of academic research, for he usually remains within a university type of organization. Moreover, he is not constrained by being identified with a highly visible policy body. Nevertheless, he pays a price for being an outsider; rarely is he able to influence the daily operations or the constituent programs of the project. The types of studies the external participant can undertake are limited.

SERENDIPITOUS PARTICIPATION

Naturally, to influence policy making is not the aim of every researcher. Many investigators find a policy role abhorrent. They contend that conducting research for policy or action purposes detracts from what they believe to be the legitimate activities of social research—that is, from basic studies of social processes and behavior. Nevertheless, their work often filters into the policy-making process. This is what is meant by "serendipitous" participation. The findings of the serendipitous policy researcher are useful to policy-making organizations only accidentally, from his point of view. For example, certain principles employed in educational programs are derived from the work of investigators who are solely concerned with understanding how children learn. Some basic research findings concerning reward and punishment have been used in therapeutic programs. A number of studies of race relations which have been used in setting social policy were conducted without reference to policy questions.

The strains and conflicts which accompany each of the roles described above will be discussed subsequently. Their categorization here permits us now to turn to a brief examination of the past and present status of social-policy research.

The Development of Social Policy Research

For a half-century or more, social scientists have been involved with social policy. The types and intensity of their involvement have varied immensely, as has their influence. American sociologists, perhaps more than other social scientists, have been attracted to their particular discipline because of their concern with social problems. As Odum (1951) points out in his analysis of the development of sociology in the

United States, a number of the important early leaders began their careers as clergymen or reformers. Some of these later turned to sociology because of their disenchantment with the prospects for achieving social change within their professions; others became sociologists because they believed that a knowledge of social behavior and social processes is essential to the management and manipulation of community life.

Many social scientists, however, even of those bent on social reform, are not interested in social policy as the term is used in this volume. Their focus has been on direct action, and their objective has been to change organizational conditions or manipulate behavior in a relatively small area or with a relatively small group of individuals (Bennis, 1963). Even so, some of their work has had an extended influence. Their efforts, seized upon and generalized, have had repercussions in many communities and on many segments of the population.

The early orientation of sociology toward action was gradually supplanted by a purportedly more scientific ideology. Increasing emphasis was placed on the importance of basic research and on the development of fundamental principles of society and social behavior. (Recently, a related movement has been championed by those who argue that major emphasis should be placed on the development of improved measuring instruments and methodological techniques.) It was not until perhaps the late 1940's that there were explicit signs of a return trend toward social reform in sociology.

THE SOCIAL-POLICY MOVEMENT

For a long time, the sociologists working on problems of immediate social concern were, in a sense, an underground movement. The movement received attention because of influential statements by young Turks who were sometimes regarded as marginal academicians.

Alvin Gouldner, a central figure in the social-policy movement (1962), examined the role of the sociologist in American society and intellectual life in a paper originally presented as his presidential address to the Society for the Study of Social Problems. He argued persuasively and with great clarity, against the tradition of objectivity, charging the value-free researcher with being socially irresponsible.

Gouldner's paper is valuable because it deals sharply with the alternative traditions in social science and social research. He specifies the need for the social researcher to be a *provocateur,* an advocate of social change and modification of values. He stresses the prerogative of the sociologist to be disrespectful of the existing social order, and maintains that the sociologist can serve an important purpose by being against the *status quo* and the establishment. Gouldner holds that concern with respectability or limitations of method and concept cannot justify a blindness to the problems of contemporary social life, and that both physical and social scientists, though they need objectivity in the operations of their investigations, cannot be morally indifferent.

Gouldner took up arms against sociologists whose primary concern was with their long-run place in their discipline, with how their colleagues would evaluate their work a quarter-century later. His primary targets were the "artistic" sociologists, wrapped up in the beauty of their work, like painters who dream of being permanently represented in the Metropolitan Museum of Art.

In contrast to the artistic sociologist, the responsibility of the social-policy type is to work in areas most directly associated with the problems of community life. He does not conceive of himself as an artist, working for future esteem, but as an agent of social change. The key role of the social-policy scientist is to mold a social order that is more consistent with human needs and human dignity. He searches for the causes of social problems and attempts to specify the conditions which will achieve a better state of affairs. He views any particular social arrangement as only one of many. Thus he often challenges the *status quo*. Perhaps most important, he asks what institutions and what courses of action are most likely to meet the needs and enhance the dignity and self-fulfillment of man.

Few social researchers, it should be noted, fall clearly in either camp. Both sets of motivations have a place in the world of scholarship and are a force in the contemporary social scene. Many social researchers mitigate the strains of a full commitment in one direction or the other by literally playing both roles: Part of the time they conceive of themselves as basic scientists; at other times they see themselves as policy researchers applying their repertoire of concepts and skills to community problems. Of course, there continue to be rather heated arguments about the proportionate expenditure of resources and the employment of time and energy which should be allocated to the one task in comparison with the other. And even those with a strong commitment to social policy do not advocate the abandonment of "basic" research. Kelman's views (1965) are representative:

> I am not proposing that social scientists devote all their time to active participation in policy formulation based on a radical analysis of institutional patterns. I am dedicated to the proposition that social scientists should feel free to pursue theoretical problems that arouse their interest, regardless of the social significance that such research might have. Similarly, I see great value in the participation of social scientists in activities related to the execution of certain policies by existing agencies. I personally engage in both of these types of activities, and intend to continue doing so (p. 39).

THE TRADITION OF POLICY RESEARCH

It was not until the 1960's that some sociologists began to explicitly demand that members of the discipline take notice of their social-policy role. However, studies of importance to policy development have a long history. It is perhaps useful to single out some specific illustrations of the kinds of inquiries that stimulated the social-policy orientation of many of those who are currently engaged in research; two illustrations will suffice.

The Western Electric Study. The work usually referred to as the Western Electric Study, or the Hawthorne Research, is described in a volume entitled *Management and the Worker* (Roethlisberger and Dickson, 1939). The findings of the study have found their way into virtually every introductory textbook in sociology and psychology, have been carefully reviewed in specialized works in industrial sociology and psychology, and have been contested a number of times (Madge, 1962).

It is unnecessary to comment here on the generality and correctness of the inferences from the Western Electric Study. The findings themselves are less important than the influence the study had in illuminating the potentialities of social research. The background of the research is succinctly reported by Madge (1962), who reviews the intertwined theoretical and pragmatic concerns which typically lead to research of a policy ilk. For some years prior to the initiation of the systematic investigations in the late 1920's, the relationship of fatigue to the productivity of workers had received considerable notice. Both in the United States and in Europe, academicians and industrialists began investigating this relationship. Their work suggested that a physiological explanation of variations in production and absenteeism was insufficient.

The Hawthorne studies came on the heels of company-initiated investigations of the effect of lighting on production. The somewhat bewildering result of the company-sponsored research was that an increase in illumination made no difference in productivity. Only later was it inferred that it was being the recipient of attention as a participant in the experiment that increased the production of the worker.

The Hawthorne research group undertook three separate studies: The first was of operations in a relay assembly test room; the second was an interview study of production-line workers and their supervisors; the third was an investigation of the social organization of a bank-wiring room.

The first was an investigation into the relationship between productivity and working conditions, a major experimental variation being the initiation of rest periods of various frequencies. While many of the specific results were problematic, the investigators made the claim, after two years of work, that the attitudes of employees were related to their productivity. This finding of a relationship between morale and productivity has been widely accepted by the general public and the industrial world. Many critiques of its generality have been offered, however, particularly during recent years (Carey, 1967).

The second study began as an interviewing program designed to obtain self-reports from employees. The interview data led to the inference that a counseling program would improve both the morale and life satisfaction of the production-line worker. It was presumed that the end-result would be an improvement in job performance. However, this assumption was never tested, so that while such counseling programs are relatively common today, their utility in improving job performance is questionable.

The third phase, the observations in a bank-wiring room, was perhaps the most sociological of the Western Electric studies. The studies of the performance of workers, as Homans (1950) has noted, pointed to the importance of informal organization and social relations in monitoring and regulating the behavior of individuals at work. The Western Electric investigators found that not only were norms of production established and controlled by the informal activities of groups, but rules of conduct were explicitly formulated on an informal level and appropriate sanctions existed for their violation.

The Hawthorne studies were carried on in one plant by two investigators with relatively modest help, yet these modest investigations had a major impact on personnel practices and management programs. Literally two generations of industrial psychologists and graduates of schools of business administration and industrial engineering, as well as many academic social scientists, have been raised on the Western Electric findings, and the investigations have had a direct impact on employees and employers in many industries.

The American Soldier. The second investigation to be described here appeared in four volumes under the general direction of Samuel Stouffer (Stouffer *et al.,* 1949, 1950, Hovland, 1949). In addition, numerous articles have been published in scholarly journals, and several books, published in the 1950's, expanded upon the results of the research.

The history of the American Soldier Research is worth scanning briefly (Madge, 1962). The program began in 1941 at the request of the Director of the Army Morale Division. He felt he could not deal with questions of morale if he had no means of discovering what the level of morale was. Stouffer was appointed director of the research unit. He had had considerable experience in applied research, and believed that research of this sort, designed for prompt use, required a continual relationship between administrators, policy makers, and researchers. He also believed that research units had to have the prerogative of anticipating problems of policy, and the capacity to work on them.

During the course of World War II, a major activity of Stouffer's group was to conduct surveys of attitudes toward jobs, Negro soldiers, civilians, leisure-time activities, and the like. About half of these surveys were undertaken in the United States, the remainder overseas. In addition, experiments in mass communication and education were undertaken. Many of the policies of the Army with respect to indoctrination and education stem from these studies. Moreover, the work of this group influenced policies concerning the separation of GI's from the armed services after the end of hostilities.

Compared to any work done up to that time, the American Soldier studies were an enormous enterprise. They were characterized, first of all, by the large number of relatively independent studies undertaken by investigators who were molded into a consortium by the administrative skill of the late Samuel Stouffer. Second, they are an early example of extensive governmental support of social research. Third, the studies were initiated by individuals charged with carrying out policy and with operations. This aspect of the research was truly innovative, because it was clearly a case where policy makers—commanding officers throughout the world—turned to the social researcher, even if only as a last resort. They wanted not only facts but also inferences and conclusions, as a basis for making decisions about the everyday life of millions of men in uniform.

As Madge (1962) notes, a major contribution of the American Soldier research was the demonstration of the utility of sophisticated techniques of analysis and the provision of an opportunity for the development and refinement of many means of quantitative analysis. This empirical work also stimulated conceptual efforts. Perhaps the best known concept developed from the studies is "reference groups" (Merton and Kitts, 1950). Many investigators have since become interested in estimating the importance of the groups with which individuals identify, as well as the groups individuals belong to, and the process by which they transfer their allegiances.

The American Soldier research has been strongly criticized, both in substance and in methodology. Perhaps the most sensitive issue raised is whether social science should be used as an instrument of mass control. Nevertheless, the research is an important illustration of the application of social science to policy, and it is a landmark, at least in terms of the magnitude of the endeavor.

Finally, the American Soldier Research deserves mention because of the composition of the research group organized by Stouffer. The team contained many of the most talented social scientists in the country, many of them fledglings whose graduate or early teaching careers were interrupted by the war. Some returned to their old jobs after World War II; others have pursued very traditional careers, combining undergraduate teaching with basic research and the training of graduate students in major universities. Many, however, were profoundly affected by their wartime experiences, because of the gratification they received from working on critical problems and the awareness they gained of the potentialities of policy making as a career. Some of the American Soldier team are now part of the elder generation of sociologists, the mentors of many of today's middle-aged policy researchers.

THE CURRENT STATUS OF POLICY RESEARCH

In the 25 years which have passed since the American Soldier studies, the social sciences have grown remarkably. Traditional activities like teaching and basic research have expanded considerably, and opportunities for applied research have mushroomed.

One purpose of emphasizing the term "social-policy research" is to filter out, from the morass of activities undertaken by sociologists, that research which is a "means," not an "end" (Angell, 1967)—that is, research which has an impact on the organization and effectiveness of major social institutions. No attempt will be made here to provide a chronology of the growth of social-policy research or to list recent important studies, although some of them will be referred to later in this volume as illustrations of the types of studies which have been undertaken.

It is fair to advise the reader that there is no assessment available of the over-all contribution of research to policy development in the fields of health, education, and welfare, although expert committees have tried to accumulate information on this matter (National Research Council, 1968; National Academy of Science, 1969). Past, current, and future policies, and the programs developed as part of them, evolve through a political process. The negotiations that ensue usually result in compromises that reflect the power, influence, and views of the key parties involved, and research is only *one* input into the policy-development process. As a recent study of the National Science Foundation (1969) noted:

> Whether or not the nation will use the social sciences in a given instance depends upon the outcome of the political competition among different vested interests, with all their degrees of approval and disapproval toward any matter at issue.
>
> The aim of the social sciences (in common with all sciences) is to seek knowledge and provide understanding, not to determine the nation's

values. This is an important point. When social science knowledge contributes to the improvement of social programs that flow from widely shared values, there is little likelihood that political controversy will occur. But when social science knowledge suggests that values should change, or that implicit values should be examined and made explicit, political controversy will almost surely arise. (p. 19–20)

In a sense then, this book is about the place research would have in social-policy development if the process of policy development occurred the way we think it should. In fact, it rarely takes place in exactly the way described. It may in many cases occur in a fashion that permits little or no contribution of a research character. But it is also fair to indicate that the recognition of the potential role of research is now widespread, a matter that merits some discussion.

Climate for Policy Research. In the fields of health, education, and welfare there is growing cooperation between policy makers and investigators. This is true even in those cases where the researcher is external to the policy body and the arena of action. Lay community leaders have also begun to appreciate the utility of policy studies, and their attitudes toward the contributions of research have changed. Notwithstanding the difficulties of carrying out policy studies, there is now in both the public and private sectors a major commitment to support social-policy research (Biderman, 1968; Williams, 1963).

The situation is remarkably different from that of two or three decades ago. The commitment of key figures to policy research is well illustrated by a sentence from Senator Walter F. Mondale's statement (1968) on the use of social indicators for policy purposes: "By bringing the best minds in social science to the question of analysis and evaluation, the President will better be able to make vital social decisions."

The political environment of the country and its philosophy regarding health, education, and welfare activities have also served to change the general view of policy research. Despite vast differences in political outlook and arguments over the execution of programs, the United States almost certainly is committed to expanding its services to the population. It is simply impossible for many types of goods and services to be purchased individually. With the development of large-scale programs in health, education, social and physical rehabilitation, welfare, and the like, the need for adequate planning, program development, and particularly evaluation is apparent to many influential community members. The stakes are so high that there is an unavoidable reliance on repeatable and explicit *modus operandi.* Thus, the role of research has increased.

Methodological and Technical Advances. Social-policy research, like all work in the social sciences, has benefited greatly from methodological and technical advances. During the last quarter-century there has been a considerable advance in research strategy, particularly in research design and the analysis of data (Blalock, 1964). In addition, computers now permit extremely rapid data processing and the widespread application of sophisticated statistical techniques to large volumes of data. Of course, improved methodology and hardware do not always insure that the quality of research will be superior. At the very least, however, improvements in method and technique have dignified the work of the social researcher and helped him to legitimize his occupational role.

The Practitioner-Researcher Relationship

The social sciences historically have maintained an affiliation with the practicing professions. Admittedly, there have been periods of considerable antagonism and hostility between social scientists and practitioners (Cottrell and Sheldon, 1963). Interpersonal barriers, including problems of communication, are one reason why the practicing professions and the social sciences have not always gotten along (Lenski, 1954). On one hand, the practicing professions are impatient with the speed of the development of knowledge and with the limited pragmatic utility of social-science research; on the other, the practicing professions have not been particularly creative about developing intellectual ideas. Moreover, the "low" status of some has impeded close working relationships with scholars. Even today, some believe that it is most difficult to bring about a close collaboration of social scientists and practitioners.

Reasons for Cooperation. In spite of the fact that there has not been a constant love match between the social researcher and members of the practicing professions, the cooperative efforts of practitioners and social scientists can be documented in a variety of fields: medical care and public health, psychiatry, social welfare, criminal law, and crime control, to name but a few. One type of engagement of sociologists with members of the practicing professions is based on the needs of practitioners for solutions to practical problems and for redefinitions of work in their fields of practice. In other instances, the social scientist has used the world of the practicing professions as a social laboratory to study problems of relevance to him from his academic standpoint. Opportunities to study work careers, interpersonal relations, organizations, and similar issues, abound; in addition, some of the more captive types of settings, such as mental hospitals, provide a ready source of subjects for many kinds of basic experimental research. In the health field, the operational types of research have been referred to as the "sociology *in* medicine," and the academic types as the "sociology *of* medicine." These two modes of work have occupied the attention of social scientists who do research in collaboration with professional colleagues or in their settings (Straus, 1957).

At times, investigations of the work of the practicing professions have stimulated policy questions. For example, the work of social researchers has been important in the development of the Medicare and Medicaid programs. Many of the recommendations of the President's Commission on Law Enforcement and Administration of Justice (1967) are derived either from completed research or from studies which were especially commissioned to examine programs in effect—the latter often "fast and dirty" ones in areas in which there was no available information.

Professional Education. The practicing professions are moving toward a greater concern with the broader social problems and the issues of social policy surrounding them. Medical educators in many schools, for example, are currently intent on broadening the perceptual field of their students and on forcing them to inquire into social process and interpersonal relations as well as into physiology and pharmacology. Many of the leaders within the health profession feel strongly that the social sciences must influence the provision of medical care now, as the life sciences have in the past. The same movement is occurring in the education of the lawyer. There has also been a radical modification of the perspectives of persons in the welfare field, from a psychoanalytic to a social-structural viewpoint.

The emerging relationships with the practicing professions provide a new source of colleagues and individuals with whom ideas can be exchanged. Traditionally, practitioners have had linkages and relationships with policy makers, and their collaborative relationships with social researchers provide a further avenue for the utilization of the findings of studies.

SOCIAL CRITICISM AND POLICY RESEARCH

Finally, the current period is one in which some social scientists feel a responsibility to be social critics and advocates for disadvantaged groups. Sometimes, their commentaries are based in part on available data, as was the brief on behalf of desegregation presented to the U.S. Supreme Court (Clark, 1955). At other times, the social scientist may be in no better position than anyone else to criticize and comment, except for the acumen which he has gained from his efforts to understand social relations and social processes. While the role of social critic is not, strictly speaking, policy research, the visibility of the social sciences has been increased by the attention paid to the observations of critical social-scientists. In general, these social critics have advanced responsible and innovative views, often modifying the ideas of policy makers (Miller and Riessman, 1968), and many of their ideas have stimulated and guided interest in policy research.

An Example of the Role of Policy Research

In discussing the role of the policy researcher, we indicated the many facets of his work and the different ways in which he relates to others in the process of policy development. Nevertheless, it is difficult to describe his day-to-day participation. The activities of the policy researcher in a comprehensive role—that is, when affiliated with a research unit—provide a clear illustration. The reader should understand that many relevant details are omitted, and, moreover, that the process of policy development has been made more orderly and apolitical than is usual in real situations.

In the early 1960's, social scientists at a federal level, collaborating with persons trained in various fields of professional practice and with the support and encouragement of the President and his White House staff, evolved a program for the control of delinquent behavior (Cloward and Ohlin, 1960). The program, which emphasized broad-scale, community-wide intervention, was based on the theory that a meaningful decrease in delinquency would occur if adolescents from low-income families were given increased opportunity to participate in the economic and social life of their communities (Cloward and Ohlin, 1960). The features of the developed program were promoted in Congress, which passed legislation authorizing demonstration programs in a number of cities.

A series of criteria was developed for the execution of the programs. A federal staff was recruited, and cities were invited to apply, on a partially competitive basis, for available demonstration funds. Subsequently, at the behest of Congress and key individuals in the executive branch of government, additional funds were provided for evaluation. This is the background for the illustration to be discussed, namely, what went on in one of the cities. Our example is hypothetical, however, since we have pooled the experiences of several cities in arriving at it.

A number of individuals with policy-making roles heard rumors about the legislation and the projected program before it was entirely structured and approved. One of these was the director of the city's delinquency-control program; another was an executive of a large voluntary agency which was interested in delinquency, among other problems. Independently, these men went to the mayor, to try to influence him to "get in on the ground floor," to obtain funds as soon as they were made available. The mayor consulted with members of the city council and other influential members of the community, and spoke with people in the health and welfare fields. He also consulted men who were important to him because of their connections throughout the city, such as some key businessmen. While these discussions were informal, nevertheless they belong under the category of planning. Not very much new information was gathered, but the mayor and the persons he consulted recognized that reducing delinquency was a relevant goal. They also agreed that a program which offered funds was a way of moving toward that goal.

The mayor, in consultation with different individuals in the community, then had to decide who should become the applicant and represent the city's fortunes in the new program. One possibility was to allow one of the major voluntary groups in the community to act on the city's behalf; another was to choose a relevant city organization, such as the police, or education or, recreation department. In the end, the mayor, in official and unofficial consultation with the city council and other important leaders, chose a third alternative. It was decided that a new, independent nonprofit body would be developed, that it would be charged with further planning, and that it would be designated as the applicant agency for the federal grant.

A small professional staff, including an associate director for research, was recruited for this independent agency. Planning in a more systematic sense now began. Since the mandate given to the professional staff was quite general and vague, the staff made many of the policy decisions themselves. They selected the area of the city to be dealt with by the new program. They determined the ability of various groups in the city to participate in the program. They submitted to the mayor recommendations for board members to oversee the work of the agency. Eventually, a board was established, with a president who was an esteemed educator with a great deal of experience in the welfare field and with children's problems.

At this point, the organization was reasonably well structured, and some of the distinctions between policy making and operations had emerged. The head of the professional staff, the executive director, remained a policy maker, as did several of his senior staff members, but many decisions were now referred to the board of the new corporation. Questions about whether to attempt a joint program with adjacent suburban areas, whether to subcontract some of the necessary research during the planning period, and where to locate offices were within the purview of the board.

Subsequent to the development of a program, a document was prepared for federal officials. It contained the outline of the program, the table of organization, and ideas about how the impact of the program on the incidence of delinquency could be evaluated. The plan included considerable information on delinquency rates, target populations, and impact models, and contained an outline of the evaluation plans. The informal submission of the plan resulted in a number of questions regarding the populations to be served, requests for refinements of the current information about delinquency, and a request for further specification of notions on evaluation.

Throughout the planning stage, and particularly during the program development stage, it was necessary for individuals responsible for program and research to meet, confer, and compromise on the programs and the evaluation procedures. The dependence of one on the other made certain types of evaluation impractical without program modifications. Certain programs were rejected because of the difficulties of developing evaluative procedures. Some program ideas stemmed from the conceptual notions of the research staff, and some of the modifications in the evaluation design were suggested by members of the planning and program group.

With the receipt of the grant to implement the program, a complex procedure of demonstration and research was initiated. A number of further modifications in plans had to be made. Estimates of available payroll funds or of available staff were not always accurate. Political pressures from the various parties involved required some shifting of ideas about programs and priorities. Commitments made by cooperating groups sometimes changed. Such modifications affected not only the programs, but the research plans as well, and some of the work originally undertaken during the planning phase had to be done over again. For example, the boundaries of the target area were shifted, which meant that additional data had to be collected, and that the indexes used to measure the different social conditions within the target area had to be recalculated.

Throughout the conduct of the program, the researchers were involved in a regular exchange with program personnel, with the executive director of the agency, and with the members of the board. The research also necessitated, and almost always received, cooperation from the various state and voluntary groups who assembled information or who had access to it: However, because such relationships are reciprocal in nature, the research staff found itself heavily involved in a broad network of activities throughout the city. Then as the program developed, it became important to obtain the cooperation of faculty members of several of the universities in the area.

Many of these persons proved to be excellent resources for the additional research assistants who were needed. Faculty members also served as consultants and provided access to important facilities, such as computers.

Soon the research group had to provide progress reports to the agencies which had supplied the funds for the project, to the board of directors, and to the many interested professionals and laymen entitled to such information, necessitating a series of descriptive and evaluative studies. Reports had to be written so that the findings would be intelligible to individuals with limited training in statistics and social research methodology.

The growing reputation of the project and its cooperative efforts with persons in local universities provided the research group with considerable prestige. There now were invitations to talk to various groups, to read papers at professional meetings, and the like. These papers were duplicated and provided to the executive director and the board of trustees of the organization.

Of course, not all the activities of the research unit could be considered social-policy research. Our sketch of life in a hypothetical action-research agency illustrates the involvement of the parties concerned, the complexities of the bureaucracy, and the variety of tasks—all of which, directly or indirectly, affected the policies of the agency.

As we have said, it is not easy to describe the role of the social-policy researcher. Our illustration should clarify some of the differences between the researcher's role when he is engaged in academic studies and when he is employed as an operational researcher. The academician on the one hand would rarely be involved in many aspects of program development. He would feel slight obligation to share his work with such a wide audience. He would be less sensitive to the need for compromises in the design; nor would he need to meet the various mandates of persons and groups in the community. Typically, the academic researcher is unsympathetic to such pressures, but even if he is not, he would rarely become professionally engaged in a community social-action program. The operational researcher, on the other hand, would be less likely to engage in what might be thought of as a "partner" relationship. Of course, some persons who consider themselves to be operational researchers initiate research and then change hats and engage in the planning and developing of programs. More often, though, the operational researcher is in a "customer-consumer" relationship. He provides services at the request and on the behalf of persons in technical and administrative roles, not policy-making ones.

In the case we have cited, the lines between the administrative and policy-making roles are not clear, nor are there sharp boundaries between social-policy research and either basic or operational research. Nevertheless there are differences, particularly when the policy researcher functions as an agent of social change. It is the spirit of the enterprise that represents the basic difference. It bears emphasis that it is misleading to portray social-policy research as a well-structured specialty. Rather, it is a developing field of activity currently characterized by the style and posture of the investigators, the types of research problems they undertake, and their concern with the social utility of their findings.

However, the social-policy orientation is certainly more than a fad. It is an increasingly dominant mode of organization of the careers of social scientists, not only in the United States. As Bryce Wood reports, "Social scientists cannot avoid being involved in the all-encompassing processes they are observing. A Brazilian participant pointed out that they cannot be neutral: 'The social scientists in Latin America have a critical attitude toward the established order; they have, on the whole, decided to help bring about transformations, and they have chosen planning as their instrument. . . . Research by social scientists must match requirements for planning and development. Otherwise, people will say professors are talking about nonexistent problems.' " (1967, p. 13.) All over the world, as Bernal (1967) notes, the trend is toward a greater consciousness of science and its position in society, and a greater awareness of its possible contribution to social reform.

The Interplay Between Policy and Research

Scientific enquiry has a long tradition as a means of understanding phenomena—physical, biological, and social. For several thousand years man has been developing and refining a set of ideas and procedures, generally referred to as the scientific method, for the discovery of knowledge and the satisfaction of his curiosity about himself and his world. Scientists share a common philosophical framework, including the fundamental beliefs that there is order in events and behavior and that that order is discoverable. Scientific enquiry requires a commitment to undertake work in conformity with a specified set of procedures and an organized means for the production of knowledge and understanding. It requires the adoption of an unbiased stand in the conduct of an investigation so as to maximize the possibility of replication; it requires a dedication to the precise definition of variables and their measurement; and finally, it must be undertaken in such a way that distortions and inaccuracies in the faulty application of techniques are minimized.

Social research is subject to the same requisites of craft and philosophy as are all other scientific endeavors. The difference is in the subject matter. In this chapter, three basic functions of scientific enquiry, and thereby of social research as well, will be discussed: description, prediction, and causal analysis. The tasks of social research in relation to policy development will also be described.

THE FUNCTIONS OF RESEARCH

All three tasks—description, prediction, and causal analysis—are vitally important to the accumulation of knowledge in the fields of social relations and social processes. Following are brief descriptions of these three important functions of research.

Description. Description is basic to all scientific enquiry; it refers to the identification of phenomena and to communications concerning their characteristics in ways that permit a sensitivity to their existence. Descriptive science deals with matters of fact, with distinctions among phenomena, and with counting and measuring them. Definitions, observation, and classification are fundamental to the descriptive enterprise. Description may consist solely of reports of the perceptions of a phenomena *in vita;* it may be based on the responses of an object to stimuli or tests; or it may include both.

Generally, two basic descriptive tasks may be distinguished: the description of the static or momentary aspects of phenomena, and the description of their dynamic or changing aspects. *Static description* deals with the reporting of observations of conditions, events, and the properties of things at a given period of time. For example, one may be interested in describing behavior which is contrary to norms or standards of a given community. *Dynamic description,* on the other hand, is the summary or interpretation of a series of two or more static descriptions relating changes that are taking place in conditions, events, or the properties of things. One might, for example, be interested in describing the types of relationships existing among two or more groups, organizations, or individuals, or the intensity of their interaction, or the degree of emotionality of the interaction, or changes in any of these.

Prediction. Scientific predictions are made either on the basis of theories (deductive prediction) or on the basis of observed relationships among variables (inductive prediction). To date, the social sciences have made only minimal progress in the production of theoretical systems with verified predictive power. Numerous efforts at inductive prediction have been made, however. The goal of inductive science is to develop a set of procedures for the collection and analysis of information so that predictions of events, conditions, characteristics, and behavior can be made. These events, conditions, characteristics, and behavior, the variables that one is interested in predicting, are called the *dependent variables;* the ones on which the prediction is based are called the *independent variables.* The variables may be quantitative or qualitative.

Inductive prediction is based on information. One type of prediction is based on rates, that is, on the relative frequency of occurrence of the phenomenon during some specified period; the other type is a statement about each individual case. For example, if it is known that approximately 10 per cent of a community's male population, 7 to 17 years of age, have been reported as delinquents in each of the past several years, both types of prediction can be attempted. One is the prediction of the delinquency rate of boys of different ages, from 7 to 17 years, in that community for one or more subsequent years; the other is the prediction of delinquency or nondelinquency of each member of the defined population during one or more periods of time. The most sensible prediction of the delinquency rate is the known rate, by age, or the average rate, of the recent past. That procedure, when used a number of times—in the attempt to predict the rates of a number of communities—will almost certainly involve much less error than any guesses made without the information. The best prediction for individuals, if the estimated community rate is 10 per cent, is a nondelinquency, since that prediction will involve only a 10 per cent error. In either case, the prediction could be improved if there were better or additional information. Better prediction means fewer errors.

Prediction in social research has not, to date, always been successful. Problems in the selection of variables and in their measurement are difficult to overcome. But the great effort being expended, the development and refinement of techniques which are taking place, and the increased opportunities afforded by the computer portend a promising future for prediction in the social sciences.

It is important to point out at this point that the ability to predict on the basis of one or more independent variables does not necessarily imply a causal connection between these independent variables (the predictor variables) and the predicted variables. The simplest example, perhaps, is the instance where the correlated variables—the independent and the dependent variables in the prediction equation—are *all* caused by some other variable or set of variables.

Causal Analysis. Causal analysis is the process of understanding the linkages among phenomena. A causal study requires that changes occur in one or more variables—either through purposeful manipulation or in the course of natural events—and that an assessment be made of the impact of these changes on one or more differentiated phenomena. Causal analyses usually include not only descriptive statements of the concomitant variation among variables and of the way one phenomenon can be modified by changes in another, but also an explanation or theory to account for the causal linkages.

The use of causal analysis in social research has evoked considerable dispute. Many individuals in the social arena, including some very vocal ones, maintain that the scientific method should not be applied to social behavior. Their point of view is an echo of critics of the biological and physical sciences. These people do not dispute the importance of description, or even of prediction, but they balk at the notion that understanding can come solely from causal experiments, arguing that an understanding of social processes and social behavior must rest on a phenomenological explanation which interprets or infers man's motives and behavior and ascribes them to the underlying basis of human nature. Most social researchers, however, have a more traditional approach and have no problem about the use of causal analysis.

Research in Relationship to Policy Development

Throughout the process of policy development—in planning, program development and evaluation—it is necessary to undertake research operations of a descriptive, predictive, and causal character. The importance of these operations varies in different aspects of policy development. In general, descriptive studies are most characteristic of the planning process; predictive studies, of program development; and causal analyses, of evaluation. In subsequent sections the various subprocesses in program development will be examined and the research tasks involved will be described in detail. Table 2.1 is a summary of the research tasks in policy development.

As indicated in Table 2.1, under Planning, descriptive data are required in order to set goals and assess existing conditions. These two tasks require information about the incidence of those conditions or behavior held to be undesirable. Information also is required about the norms with which the data are contrasted. In parentheses, under Planning, one finds the task of developing an action strategy. *Strategy* here means the first approximation of the impact model and the selection of the target population, which are discussed at some length later in this book. In the stage of Program Development and Execution, when the impact model is developed, both prediction and causal analysis are relevant research tasks. Ideally, the development of an impact model should depend heavily on causal studies, but this is rarely the case. Most impact models are based primarily on predictive investigations. The selection of a target population usually involves both descriptive and predictive analysis. Under Evaluation, the assessment of the program's execution is shown as a descriptive task; it involves the comparison of the actual program, as conducted, with the design. Measuring the impact requires the conduct of experiments. While the chapters which follow do not exhaust the research tasks involved, they do describe these major activities of policy-oriented investigators.

TABLE 2.1

Research in Policy Development

	Research Tasks		
	Description	*Prediction*	*Causal Analysis*
Planning:			
Setting goals	X		
Assessing existing conditions	X		
(Developing an action strategy)		X	X
Program Development and Implementation:			
Developing an impact model		X	X
Selecting the target population	X	X	
Evaluation:			
Assessing the implementation program	X		
Measuring its impact			X

Chapter 3

RESEARCH AND PLANNING

In our discussion of the planning process, it was pointed out that planning almost always involves the use of research information for contrasting the way things are with the way things should be, that is, to explicate the socially desirable goals and to assess the extent of deviations from them. This process of looking at what exists in comparison with what is construed to be desirable can only be accomplished if the planner has a yardstick, that is, some measurement of the behavior or condition he is addressing. At first glance, developing yardsticks for measuring social behavior and community conditions may appear simple. It is not; moreover, the success of program planning depends upon the selection of relevant measures.

Choice of Measures

Since facts are often easy to come by, the astute planner can be distinguished by his ability not to be overwhelmed by information. Planners, of course, make use of their own experiences in judging the state of affairs in a community. But a single individual rarely has a complete and unbiased view of social conditions and behavior, and he must also make use of systematic information. Moreover, the planner almost always must make his case, either to the political structure, his policy board, or the constituency involved. In his use of data, he needs on the one hand to have the relevant information; on the other, he needs to be sparing in what he collects and careful in how he assembles and presents it.

Some psychologists, in trying to understand why certain people do not function very well, talk about "information overload." The idea is that it is possible to become confused, disturbed, and immobilized by knowing too much as well as too little. Policy researchers thus often seek to reduce the data on hand in order to cut down on the number of disparate figures they are dealing with. This is one of the reasons persons in the health field resort to measures such as the number of days hospitalized or the frequency of physicians' visits, rather than to individual diagnoses, when they are estimating the health of a population. It allows them to use a single figure rather than a long list of information.

Compiling data and reducing the amount of information is not often easy in important policy areas. With the exception of information of an economic character, there are limitations to the feasibility of combining different descriptive measures. It is important to recognize that reduction of measures can distort or conceal certain types of deviations from expected standards. For example, persons interested in problems of crime and delinquency control may be falsely complacent or overexcited about conditions in a particular community if their planning is based upon an over-all rate of court appearances rather than on rates of conviction for particular crimes. One community might have 25 murders and little else, and another may have only 100 convictions for drunkenness. The technical problems involved in reducing information are extensive. What is usually required is the identification of an underlying dimension or continuum on which different phenomena can be placed.

There is no entirely satisfactory solution to the problem of developing comprehensive measures. One common approach has already been mentioned, the conversion of the data into some common "resource measure." The most common resource measure is dollars, into which many types of behavior and conditions can be converted. For example, rather than the incidence of illnesses and accidents of factory workers, dollars of income lost may be used. Or information may be converted into a measure of manpower, such as lost hours of productive work.

A second approach is to conceptualize and empirically develop an underlying ordinal continuum. This is what Sellin and Wolfgang (1964) did in developing their seriousness-of-delinquency scale. They attempted to estimate the seriousness of delinquency by developing a scale that would give different weights to different delinquent acts, the weights being based upon the severity with which legal officials responded to them. The theft of an automobile hubcap in their scheme, therefore, would be given much less weight than the armed robbery of a person in his house.

Which solution one selects depends both on technical matters and on the researcher's view of the ease of communication to lay persons. This matter of communication is one of the reasons why so much information is expressed in economic terms.

Aggregation and Disaggregation

At the same time that it is desirable to reduce descriptive data to a small set of indicators, their value depends upon how readily they can be aggregated or disaggregated. "Aggregation" and "disaggregation" are technical terms. The reduction of a myriad of rates into a single measure is one form of aggregation, as is Sellin and Wolfgang's seriousness-of-delinquency scale (1964) which pools data about a variety of illegal acts into a single measure. Another, more common, form of aggregation is the pooling of the same kind of data about different groups collected at different times or places. For example, one may aggregate into a single figure, data about murder rates in all cities of over 1,000,000 people.

The process of disaggregation is the converse, namely, sorting out the data into data about various attributes of individuals, groups, and communities. For example, if a planner hopes to reduce by half the number of children arrested for illegal behavior in his state, he would probably be foolish not to obtain data disaggregated by sex as well as by several social and community characteristics.

Too much disaggregation is as immobilizing and useless as too little. The astute policy researcher must know enough about the mechanics of planning in a particular field so that in his collection and analytical treatment of descriptive data he minimizes the undesirable consequences of both under and overdisaggregation. For example, if a program is to provide services within counties, then state data that cannot be disaggregated into county data is of limited utility. Conversely, if a program must by law or local custom be available to all without reference to religion, then data disaggregated by religion is an exercise in futility. The ability to come up with the right set of descriptive statistics and to be economical in the specification of variables is something the policy investigator learns experientially. There are no rules. He must know his planners, he must know his organization, and he must be sensitive to the ramifications of the social problems that are the focus of the action effort.

Sources of Data

Researchers should try to avoid the collection of new data during the planning process. Field studies are exceedingly costly, and require a major commitment of personnel. Moreover, there is a long wait for the results. Finally, efforts to speed up the research, or economize, almost invariably result in studies so incompetent that it would have been better not to have made them at all. At best, in comparison to academic studies, social policy investigations are subject to close tolerances in terms of time and often of financial resources.

The expense of a planning study is related to the frequent need for multiple cross-classifications of information. For example, an analysis of a sample of 5,000 individuals representing the population of a large city school system may be sufficient for drawing over-all conclusions. But if it is necessary to disaggregate the data by race, census tract, and several other variables, there will be too few cases in each category to permit meaningful interpretations of the various combinations of characteristics.

Both policy makers and fledgling researchers must be warned that the collection of data is not an inexpensive enterprise. A decent household interview and its processing costs between $25 and $50, perhaps more. If the number of cases is large or if new instruments must be designed and tested, this adds to the cost and takes more time. Few investigations report results within a year of their inception.

The Use of Collected Data

While it is not possible for any one individual to be fully conversant with the range of publications and sources of secondary data—that is, data which have already been collected and processed—researchers must be at least familiar with the common sources. Perhaps the most valuable single volume is the yearly publication, *Statistical Abstract of the United States* (U.S. Department of Commerce, 1969). It is useful for its many tables, the cited sources of which also frequently lead to additional material.

One of the skills that the social-policy researcher does not learn in college or university is to play detective, to identify individuals and organizations with access to the descriptive data he needs. In the same way as an academically-oriented researcher needs colleagues and access to research reports which may never be published or may be published years after his study is completed, policy researchers need relationships with the persons and agencies that collect and process descriptive data.

The most obvious source of secondary data may not be the best one. In one Central-American country, for example, a policy-oriented research group that required data about the composition of communities found it easier and faster to visit the mayors of small towns and use local information than to attempt to extract the material from the national census bureau. In a study involving union membership, the insurance carrier handling the industry's health plan proved to be a better source of data about members than the union itself.

It may be less challenging and intellectually stimulating to locate and analyze secondary data than to design field studies, but the general rule is that new field investigations should only be undertaken after the search for secondary sources has been exhausted or when the available data is too imprecise to yield the necessary estimates. In estimating the utility of secondary data in planning, the researcher must take into account the quality of the material, a technical matter which will be examined in a subsequent chapter.

Social Indicators

Particularly at the national level, the need for descriptive data in the planning activities of the various government groups is great. At the present time, many different federal agencies prepare and publish data about rates in the areas of their responsibility. Often their measures summarize information contributed by local and state groups, as do the F.B.I. crime reports. Sometimes they arise from specially commissioned studies done within the government or by private groups. Universities and other groups also contribute to the supply of national or regional information. There are a number of criticisms of the existing situation, including duplication of effort, insufficient concern with the quality of the data, and the limited opportunities to disaggregate the information.

Because of the special value of longitudinal data that permit the plotting of trends, there have been numerous proposals to establish a series of comprehensive social indicators. In 1967, hearings were held on a Social Accounting Act, which would have set up an authority to be known as the Council of Social Advisors. A major responsibility of this Council would have been to accumulate, integrate, and analyze data so that the progress of the country could better be estimated and those problems of most concern and priority identified (U.S. Congress, 1967).

There have been several volumes on the development of social indicators (Bauer, 1966; Gross, 1967; Moore and Sheldon, 1968). Part of the interest in social indicators stems from the desire to be able to compare particular social conditions or behavior at different times and to estimate rates of change. Another reason for the interest is the desire of social-policy researchers and policy makers alike to be able to gauge the "state of the nation" over periods of time and with respect to groups and communities with different characteristics. Ideally, some say, it would be desirable to have a series of indicators which could be accumulated so as to obtain a single net figure, like one sees in an accountant's balance sheet. If this could be done, it would be possible to evaluate the social affairs of the country as a whole, of parts of it, or of groups in it from year to year, in much the same way that a businessman estimates his success or failure for the year or judges how different departments in his store are doing. As a matter of fact, the federal government and many state and local governments do just that in terms of the economic situation, although it is not possible now to develop a set of social accounts.

Social indicators, at both the national and local levels, would be valuable in the development of goals and objectives, although in themselves they cannot provide goals and objectives. As we have pointed out, however, goals and objectives are often set when the empirical condition is known. One purpose of a set of social indicators is to force the policy maker to examine various conditions and types of behavior and to compare the current situation with the past.

Data Banks and Information-Retrieval Systems

With the development of computers and the acceleration of special studies, either for general scholarly interest or as part of the social-policy research endeavor, considerable attention has been devoted to the establishment of "data banks." Storage systems on a national level, for example, might pool results of large numbers of regional and local studies on the same topics and problems. Those developed at a metropolitan, state, or regional level would consolidate studies undertaken on a variety of issues so that data from them can be pooled. Investigators would benefit from comparing their findings with data stored in the bank, and the existence of the data in the banks would encourage more consistency in the wording and type of items used in studies. Consequently, data banks promise a continual refinement of information without necessitating special studies. Data banks exist in less than complete form in a number of metropolitan areas, and many groups and agencies are seeking to develop them for special purposes. Although few were specifically designed for social-policy research, they have much to offer the planner as ready sources of data for descriptive studies.

Closely linked, and perhaps somewhat more developed, are the information-retrieval systems which readily permit the acquisition of references and information already reported in the research literature. In many fields, including health, mental illness, poverty, and the like, computer-based information services provide all sorts of information, including descriptive information, literally in seconds. One of the earliest and more refined of these services is part of the National Library of Medicine. Its system provides a dictionary-type listing of various topics, and the researcher or policy maker may request any material listed in an item or combination of items in the dictionary (U.S. Department of Health, Education, and Welfare, 1966). He may ask for studies on the incidence of syphilis among subgroups of the population, for example, and if such studies have been published they will be provided through the Library.

The rapid development of data banks and retrieval systems, on one hand, supplies the social-policy researcher with enormously greater and broader quantities of data than he has previously had available. On the other hand, the sophistication of the policy maker himself becomes even more important. Assembling and using large quantities of data often require unusual astuteness and perseverance.

Incidence and Prevalence

The planner, as we noted earlier, almost always finds data most useful if they are expressed in rates. A rate is a statement of an occurrence expressed in unit terms. The planner is much better able to render judgments if he knows not only that there are 500 dilapidated dwellings, but that this constitutes 8 dwelling units per 100 in the community. This latter is an example of a prevalence rate; it should not be confused with an incidence rate. There is a real distinction between incidence and prevalence.

Incidence refers to the occurrence of a phenomenon during a specified period, to the onset of a situation. Incidence figures usually have meaning, however, only when onset or occurrence is indicated in relation to the potential pool of persons or situations which might have been affected. Thus, the incidence of poliomyelitis, the number of cases detected within a particular period, is expressed in relation to the size of the population. Ten new cases of polio have differing significance in Cedar Rapids than in New York City.

Prevalence refers to the number of cases of a particular phenomenon in a community or group at a given time. Prevalence figures also are most useful only if there is also a statement which includes information about the population at risk. Thus "the prevalence rate of poliomyelitis" is the number of individuals with the disease at a particular time, as compared with the total population (MacMahon, 1960).

The Importance of the Denominator. The complexities of measuring incidence and prevalence are many. Who, for instance, should be included in the denominator? The general principle is indicated in the phrase "population at risk." Ideally, the denominator should include all potentially vulnerable individuals, but information about them is often not available and a less perfect denominator must be employed. For example, in measuring the incidence of venereal disease, only sexually active persons should be counted; since this information is not available, an age group of persons who are likely to be sexually active is used instead. It is easy to see that estimates of the seriousness of a problem can depend on how the denominator is handled.

The Choice between Incidence or Prevalence Figures. How does one decide whether it is incidence or prevalence that is important? If we are dealing with the problem of heroin and morphine addiction, the figure of most concern is prevalence. Not very many new addicts are produced in a day, a week, or a month, and our lack of success in treating the disorder makes the prevalence figure the one that merits scrutiny. In investigating delinquency, however, our concern is essentially with incidence; it would be foolish to believe that "once a delinquent, always a delinquent." The important figure is the number of delinquent acts committed during a specified time within a given population.

The issue of whether it is prevalence or incidence that is important frequently becomes much more knotty, however. There is debate about whether mental illness in a community should be judged in terms of prevalence or incidence. Given new methods of treatment, much shorter hospitalizations, and expanded community mental-health services, more and more attention is being focused on incidence figures. Increasingly, the assumption in mental-health care is that the important task is to minimize the number of new cases.

In many instances, both types of data are important and need to be provided. However, many persons, particularly laymen involved in policy decisions, do not understand either the difference between incidence and prevalence or the intricacies involved in constructing rates. It is the researcher's responsibility, therefore, to make certain that the rates he develops reflect the situation accurately.

Differences in Visibility and Processing. Rates are only as good as the data on which they are based. A major complexity in the estimation of phenomena stems from the differences in the visibility of actions and consequently, in the processing of cases. Crime affords a clear illustration of the point. It appears that only a small proportion of criminals are apprehended. Therefore, information about the incidence of crime obtained from law-enforcement agencies is highly problematic. Furthermore, descriptive data is often most useful if the rates in various geographical areas or among different types of persons can be compared. Statistics about crime again illustrate the problem. From city to city, there is variation in the informal policies of the police, and they thus may be more, or less, inclined to arrest and hold the adolescents, first offenders, and those accused of certain types of crime. There is also reason to believe that justice operates differentially, depending upon the background of the offender (Wald, 1967).

Often, only the most creative and extensive approaches can overcome the problems of differences in visibility and processing. In most instances, however, it is possible to improve the descriptive data available. Thus, the President's Commission on Law Enforcement and Administration of Justice (1967), in order to provide more accurate information on criminal activities than might be gleaned from official data on reported crime, conducted a public-opinion poll in which community members were asked whether or not they had been confronted with criminal activity during a specific period. Not only was the reported volume of crime much higher than the police information indicated, but the relative frequencies of different criminal acts varied greatly from those reported in the official statistics.

Rates and Goal Setting. Incidence and prevalence figures are more than measures of existing conditions. To the policy maker, they are a point of reference, a basis for evaluating the desirability of present conditions. Rates sensitize the planner to what should be done. Sometimes his judgment is based on moral or ethical values, as when the sexual conduct of high-school students is under study. At other times, it is based on economic or social cost, as when he is concerned about automobile accidents. At still other times, a judgment of undesirability is associated with beliefs about the stability and functioning of organizations and social institutions. In all these cases, however, there are no absolute norms. The judgment that some particular incidence or prevalence level is too high or low often follows, rather than precedes, knowledge of the existing state of affairs.

Planners are not the only ones who go through the process of first looking at what exists and then reaching a view about what is desirable. Individuals and organized groups in the community do the same thing, and their knowledge of an existing situation often results in confrontations with policy-making bodies. In this way, community members help to institute and stimulate planning. The availability of rates in different groups or areas often is most valuable in this respect. For example, high-school dropout rates (usually an incidence figure) may alert both educators and local residents to problems in the schools. The contrasting of different rates is an important reason to be concerned with the selection of appropriate denominators and with some of the other matters we have been discussing.

COMPILATION OF DESCRIPTIVE DATA

Both cross-sectional and periodically collected descriptive data have their uses in planning. A single incidence or prevalence rate is an illustration of *cross-sectional data*. The planner concerned with setting goals or judging deviations from them may wish to have at his fingertips a large number of figures for a single period of time, about different problems, or from different groups or areas. However, policy development usually is a continuing process, as we have noted. Few planners are comfortable unless they can compare the state of affairs over a longer period of time. Prevalence or incidence rates for the same behavior or condition at two points in time, may be thought of as a "time-series." Time series provide a means for estimating either progress or the lack of amelioration of a social problem. Such data may also suggest what behavior or condition that was relatively dormant suddenly requires attention.

The compilation of both cross-sectional and longitudinal data involves technical and substantive choices. The researcher involved in the planning process must decide how much data should be collected and analyzed, and in how much detail; he must balance the advisability of presenting large numbers of specific measures against the possibility of using a smaller number of comprehensive ones; and he must consider whether to use over-all population data or data about different groups in the population. In addition, as we have said, the researcher needs to locate sources of data and decide whether to collect new data or use secondary information, balancing the cost and speed of the research operation against the often unknown precision and accuracy of secondary information.

The Risks of Bias

The social researcher who is engaged in providing special descriptive data or in reviewing secondary information must be aware of the need to avoid the bias which accrues from his obligations to individuals with whom he is affiliated or from values he is seeking to promote.

Perhaps no single field illustrates the issues that surround the drawing of inferences from descriptive data more sharply than the study of the nonwhite community member in the United States. Data disaggregated by race point up most dramatically the inequities in housing, education, and employment. Most policy makers who advocate programs that provide greater equity and opportunity for the Negro are therefore on the side of those who plead for the accumulation and presentation of data by skin color. However, data on race are often regarded as detrimental to the image of the Black (reporting crimes by race is an illustration), and efforts are also made to eliminate the collection of such information. In general, appeals to conceal differences are impetuous and emotional, and are likely to be regretted later. Consider, for example, how difficult planning would be if census data could not be disaggregated by race. Nevertheless, it is not possible to be entirely immune to arguments for minimizing social differences by simply avoiding their identification. Clearly, there needs to be a convincing rationale for maintaining data disaggregated by different social characteristics.

Another aspect of the problem of bias is the fact that policy makers often have to accept the interpretations and inferences of research-trained persons. Quite simply, the policy makers may have technical limitations or may lack the time and energy to undertake a close scrutiny of the data themselves. For example, individuals involved in the development of family planning programs at a policy level, such as public health officials, directors of welfare agencies, and chiefs of obstetric centers, generally have limited training in demography. The statistical information about their own communities and the national scene is usually processed, analyzed, and interpreted by others. These policy makers, therefore, are almost entirely dependent upon demographers in reaching judgments with respect to the planning of new programs, and how would they know if the demographers were biased?

Several guidelines can be offered to curtail biases. First, the researcher must recognize that, while he may wish to influence the values and decisions of policy makers by persuading them to regard things as he does, his views should not deter him from presenting an unbiased and objective analysis. It would be inconsistent with his role as a researcher for him to use his ability and technical knowledge as tricks of persuasion.

Second, the social researcher must resist providing policy makers with marginally relevant data merely because of tradition or his personal sociological interests. It is important that data be disaggregated so that their implications are as sharp as possible. Yet there is an infinite set of permutations and combinations of measures. Policy development is impeded when bias is accidentally or purposefully introduced into the thinking of the policy maker by an inappropriate selection of variables for disaggregation.

Third, the social researcher must carefully estimate the degree of sophistication of those with whom he is dealing in the policy-making process. To the extent that they are unsophisticated about the techniques and craft of the social researcher, his responsibility is to make clear the limitations and pitfalls of his data. The researcher must also protect his data from misuse. He must accept primary responsibility for the actions stemming from his input of information.

Finally, the social researcher must recognize that policy makers, often with good intentions, inappropriately use research data as a means of influencing their colleagues or influential members of the community. The researcher has a responsibility, both to the policy organization and to the broader collectivity of scientists, to avoid engaging in such activities and, indeed, to protest their occurrence when he becomes unwittingly involved in them.

The policy researcher, then, must strive to minimize the biases accruing from insufficient resources, faulty techniques, and his own extensive engagement in the planning operation.

THE ASSESSMENT OF GOALS

In the discussion of descriptive data for planning, the point has been made that the availability of empirical information about behavior and conditions influences the goals set by policy makers. In particular, rates and other information of a comparative character provide yardsticks valuable in the specification of goals. The researcher has additional means of providing the policy maker with systematic information useful in establishing goals. Planners typically do not look upon themselves as goal setters, but rather as interpreters of community conditions and values. Their explication of standards is to a large extent a political venture, an attempt to balance diverse views and to point relevant groups and organizations in a direction that will maximize their well-being, often by compromising differences.

In addition to the objective situation, therefore, planners must be sensitive to the values held by members of the community. Like them, planners also derive many of their ideas about goals from the underlying set of moral norms referred to as "Judeo-Christian ethics"; but they are also aware of expert opinion in many fields, of views derived either from scientific study or experiential wisdom. These too are involved in the goal-setting process. Third, planners often must take into account what sociologists call "subjective" or "attitudinal" norms, that is, information about how persons feel things *should* be done, whether or not they actually behave that way themselves. The social investigator can offer suggestions to the policy maker who uses any of these aids in establishing goals and standards. Indeed, some individuals within the social sciences argue that wisdom and skill can be used more appropriately in the setting of goals than in any other way (Ranney, 1968).

INTERPRETING SOCIAL VALUES

Sociologists and anthropologists, in the normal course of their academic work, pay particular attention to the social values and the ethical and religious heritages of their own culture (Williams, 1951). Our values are linked together, interdependent within a complex matrix, and it is both an empirical and conceptual task to unravel them. This process of specifying, or at least hypothesizing, the interdependencies is crucial if goals are to be established rationally. The point can be illustrated quite simply: Most people would agree that the prolongation of life and the maximum provision of health services is an important social value which should guide the setting of goals for public health. At the same time, our heritage demands that we maximize opportunities for community members to assert themselves and to realize their desires to participate in political and social decisions. There are grounds to argue that activities of the latter sort, concerted and vigorous social protests, are maximum only when there is extreme dissatisfaction and frustration. Therefore, efforts to approximate goals in the health area may serve to reduce dissatisfaction and frustration and may counteract movement towards greater community expression in social and political areas.

Policy makers are unlikely to rely solely upon persons trained in the social-science disciplines to estimate the interactive effects of decisions to promote a particular goal or standard. Yet the trained social-scientist does have the responsibility, as well as some technical competence, to specify for the policy maker the interrelationships among values. He is also in a position possibly to estimate the consequences of giving priority to one value rather than another in the development of goals and standards (Herring, 1965).

Unfortunately, much of the academic work on the matrix of values has not been directly useful in policy development (Loomis, 1960). But an emerging area of work for the social scientist and social researcher is the sorting out of the various ends that a policy is designed to pursue in relation to the expenses that are likely in terms of other social values (Millikan, 1959).

COLLATING EXPERT VIEWS

Many policy makers have their own group of experts to whom they turn for opinions on appropriate standards. Others make use of a more extensive network, experts who more broadly represent the range of available ideas. Particularly in framing public programs, legislative and regulatory bodies often insist upon the formal and representative selec-

tion of experts. One task of the social researcher is to solicit, in a systematic, methodologically rigorous manner, the views of the relevant
parties or those so designated by the policy body. In this sense, the social
researcher is applying some of his tools of interviewing and data analysis
to a specialized sample.

The views of experts, however, are rarely congruent with each
other, and so the social researcher can contribute to another policy task.
He can use his skills to account for variations in the views of experts.
The diversity of their views may arise either because of the characteristics of the experts themselves, the experiences they have had in the past,
or their organizational affiliations. It is obvious, for example, that ideas
about the desirability of different types of television programs are going
to vary, depending upon whose expert opinion is solicited. People in
advertising, in the broadcasting industry, and in education are going to
hold opinions which are somewhat related to their occupational and economic situations.

Analyses of variations in expert views and the characteristics associated with these variations can provide insight to the policy maker
seeking to compromise or rationalize a particular position with respect
to goals. In certain areas, because of the crucial or sensitive character of
the problem, considerable effort has been expended to systematically collect, analyze, and differentiate the views of experts. Most of this work
requires technical skills in the collection and analysis of data that are
rarely available except from those with social-research training.

IDENTIFYING NORMS AND ATTITUDES

Both a position on social values and a pragmatic concern underlie
the interest of policy makers in the norms and attitudes of the general
run of community members, particularly of those persons who may be
directly affected by policies. An old fear of planning, at least of broad-
scale planning, is based on the possibility that autocratic decisions may
be made by a select few and that a new totalitarian aristocracy will
eventually develop. Only partly because of this fear, there is a widespread view among planners that planning in a democracy must take into
account, some say must be determined by, the views of the parties involved. Certainly it is important to develop mechanisms which allow
broad participation in setting goals (Rothwell, 1951).

The pragmatic consideration is that goals which are inconsistent
with the behavior or antagonistic to the beliefs of a significant proportion
of the affected group are usually exceedingly difficult to carry out. Furthermore, if policy makers deem it crucial to promote goals which
arouse antagonism—as, for example, to eliminate cigarette smoking—they

must be aware of the nature and sources of the antagonism. In other words, the characteristics of the population affect the development of an efficacious program strategy. The concern is often with the actual behavior of the parties affected, but it may also be with the expressed beliefs or attitudes of persons.

There are many opinions about the setting of goals in relation to the *objective norms,* i.e., that which exists, and the *subjective norms,* i.e., that which people believe or feel. It is difficult, within the scope of this volume, to expand upon the diversity of these views or to derive any principles. A couple of illustrations will perhaps be useful, however. Contrast, for example, the situation in a community where there is only a single mode of conduct that most people follow with one in which there are variant patterns of behavior. In order to set a goal in the first instance, it must be decided how great a departure from the dominant pattern will be tolerated by the persons involved. To set a goal in the second situation, one must determine whether conflicting reactions will arise.

Consider the difference between attempting to eliminate heroin addiction and alcohol addiction. In the case of heroin, the goal can be stated most simply: to eliminate all use except under a physician's surveillance. Given the many divergent drinking patterns, however, how does one state the goal in the case of alcohol? It is easy to see that the attitudes of the persons affected must be an important concern of the policy maker as he sets goals during planning (Freeman and Scott, 1966).

The social researcher's assessment of both the subjective and objective norms may depend entirely upon secondary analyses of data already collected. He may, however, undertake field studies himself. The entire array of methods of data collection, and many of the stipulations about them mentioned in the discussion of rates, apply to the assessment of norms. Here, as well as in determining rates, the scientific orientation and the technical repertoire of the social researcher are valuable to the planning process.

THE PROBLEM OF PRIVACY

One needs to be concerned about personal rights and privacy—and we shall return to this point later in the book. The very process of collecting and storing descriptive data without the knowledge and permission of the parties involved constitutes an invasion of individual privacy. The question in social planning is not whether research operations violate privacy, for many of them do. Rather, the issues are whether it is worth it, and whether maximum safeguards have been taken to protect the individual.

Some social researchers advocate a national data bank in which large quantities of information about all individuals in the United States would be stored, and in which social security numbers would be used for identification. Such a compilation of data from federal, state, local, public, and voluntary groups could provide a comprehensive dossier on "typical" Americans which would be most useful in planning as well as in program development. The proponents of a national storage system strongly argue the value of having large amounts of information about individuals readily available. While the establishment of a national file on each and every American is at best a long way off, the risks attending the accumulation of data about individuals are well worth our concern (Sawyer and Schechter, 1968).

Undoubtedly, one of the greatest safeguards against the misuse of data is the integrity of the social researcher himself. It should be emphasized that social-policy researchers who accumulate descriptive data must take care, at each and every step of the operation, whether or not undertaken by the researchers themselves, to ensure the privacy of the individuals involved.

Mutual respect, and the increasing status of the social researcher has the side-effect of increasing the cooperation of relevant parties. While this is all to the good, there are times when the social researcher has information that may cause embarrassment, loss of employment, or unhappiness, although he may never intend to use it. Cooperative police departments often are willing to provide data about crimes and delinquencies, including names for example, and mental hospitals and departments of public health give out information about persons with different illnesses, including their characteristics and the like. The researcher's responsibility in this regard is a serious one.

Concluding Comment

In this chapter we have introduced some technical ideas about measurement and tried to relate the use of research—primarily descriptive research—to planning. Our point is that the planning process proceeds rationally only when data on conditions and norms are available to the planner.

Chapter 4

RESEARCH AND PROGRAM DEVELOPMENT

Some preliminary steps in program development, at least of a speculative kind, are usually undertaken simultaneously with planning. There comes a point, however, when the policy-development group is required to be explicit and specific about the means to be used to achieve change or modification.

Ideally, the policy makers and practitioners who are brought in to help design programs should accord the highest priority to the development of an impact model. Unfortunately, this is usually not the case. Too often they simply fail to recognize the importance of specifying an impact model. They are frequently unable or reluctant to specify an impact model for programs which is both repeatable and generalizable. They have difficulty in communicating exactly what they do in various programs, particularly when interpersonal skills are integral to the effort. And in some cases, there may be an unconscious or even a conscious fear that the explication of an impact model will reveal the superficiality of the projected program. Nevertheless, it is impossible either to duplicate a program or to evaluate it unless an impact model is provided. (Borgatta, 1959).

It is likely to require pressure from the policy researcher to get the policy and practitioner groups to come up with a sufficiently explicit impact model. Many times, the researcher finds himself doing most or all

55

of the work, and not until he presents his understanding of the program do the practice-oriented persons respond with corrections and clarifications. The social researcher who has a comprehensive role in the program can, unlike researchers in more limited roles, keep a dialogue going with persons engaged in program development and execution until some explicit agreement is reached on the impact model.

ELEMENTS IN THE IMPACT MODEL

The impact model, as we have previously noted, is a statement about the expected relationships between a program and movement toward a goal. The impact model is the statement of the strategy for closing the gap between the standard or goal that is set during the planning process and the existing behavior or condition. It must contain a causal hypothesis, an hypothesis about the intervention, and an action hypothesis.

The Causal Hypothesis. At the heart of any impact model is a hypothesis about the influence of one or more characteristics or processes on the condition which is the object of the program. The hypothesis assumes a causal relationship between a phenomenon and the condition or behavior in which a change is sought.

There are a number of different ways of thinking about cause, and we will discuss them subsequently. Here, a simple idea of cause may suffice. Many social scientists believe, for example, that there is a relationship between anomie and deviant social conduct. A number of investigators (Gibbs, 1966) maintain that a lack of integration between an individual and the social structure is a primary cause of suicide. A causal hypothesis, then, would be that suicide will be directly related to one's integration with the social structure. But in order to have utility, all hypotheses, including causal ones, have to be stated in a way that permits of their testing. (This is the process of operationalization.) The social researcher, in particular, would probably strain to restate his hypothesis in a way which could be measured. He might do it this way: Suicide is most likely among persons who participate least in their community's political activities and voluntary associations, and whose contacts with their families and other intimates are limited in both number and intensity.

An important point to grasp is that *both* anomie and suicide would have to be measured in the subsequent evaluation. Therefore, part of the task of developing an impact model is to specify the variables, either in terms of some measure or in a way which permits them to be defined operationally.

The Intervention Hypothesis. The intervention hypothesis is the statement which specifies the relationship between the program (what is going to be done) and the phenomenon regarded, in the causal hypothesis, as associated with the behavior or condition to be ameliorated or changed. The intervention hypothesis, in our example, might be that a knowledge of community resources and organizations is related to participation in political and voluntary groups. A program would then be specified to increase the spread of knowledge of these resources and organizations. Thus, the impact model for the reduction or prevention of suicide would specify that a program to increase the spread of knowledge of resources and organizations will lead to increased social and political participation (less anomie), which will lead to a reduction in suicide. But a third hypothesis, at a minimum, is required.

The Action Hypothesis. The action hypothesis is necessary in order to assess whether the intervention, even if it results in a desired change in the causal variable, is necessarily linked to the outcome variable, that is, the behavioral condition that one is actually seeking to modify. This third hypothesis is necessary because, although the chain of events may be a true one in real life, it may not necessarily hold when it has been brought about by intervention. The introduction of change may not be the equivalent of the behavioral and social processes that exist naturally. When an action is planned, different conditions are present. In our case, increasing people's participation in community activities through an educational program may not make them any less prone to suicide than before, despite an existing relationship between anomie and suicide in the population as a whole.

In an interesting piece of research on this matter, causal links are presumed between (1) understanding and knowledge of Negroes and (2) prejudice, on the one hand, and between prejudice and (3) discrimination, on the other. A program was developed for employment managers, to increase (1) their understanding and knowledge, so as to decrease (2) their prejudice. The odd result of the program was that those employment managers whose attitudes (2) changed the most discriminated (3) *more* than they had before. Festinger (1964) explained this result by arguing that the input of new information led to a polarization of behavior. In other words, in the face of the program, it was impossible for the employment managers to continue behaving as before. Therefore, while some of them became less discriminatory, others became more so in their hiring practices. Neither the findings of the study nor Festinger's explanation vitiates the causal links that exist in the normal course of socialization: the point is that even if things happen in a natural state, we may not be able to induce them. The action hypothesis is therefore as important as the other hypotheses in policy investigations and needs to be studied empirically.

CAUSAL MODELS

In discussing the hypotheses required in the specification of an impact model, we took a most simple explanation or view of causation, presuming linear, direct links between three phenomena or variables. Researchers are well aware that the causal sequence of events is rarely so simple (Duncan, 1966). While a thorough examination of concepts of causality is impossible here, a brief discussion of several alternatives may be useful.

Multi-causal Models. As most readers are aware, there is little social behavior and few social conditions which can be accounted for by a single cause. It is quite possible that a number of entirely independent causes exist. For example, an automobile accident may be caused by improper driving, a faulty automobile, and bad weather. However, such a statement of multi-causality can represent an incomplete or sloppy unraveling of the links among the various phenomena. Bad weather may cause improper driving, because the probability that individuals will drive off the sides of roads is greater in fog and rain. In the development of the impact model, the question of whether multiple causes are interdependent or independent should be examined. If they are interdependent, the complications must be taken into account both in the causal hypothesis and the hypothesis about intervention.

In most cases, the identification of correlates of the various phenomena under study, as well as the presumptions and inferences made about cause, suggest the utility of a number of specific program developments. This is so not only because many factors are believed to be involved in the etiology of the phenomenon under attack, but also because of a reluctance to put the entire effort into a single program. And with the extended application of programs of a comprehensive character which involve a large number of different intervention activities, interaction between various program elements usually occurs. These interactions require the development of complex impact models, but unless it is possible to unravel all of the stages and sequences in the execution of the program, evaluation cannot take place.

Impact models help us to recognize possible duplication of efforts and services. Some of the Office of Economic Opportunity's "comprehensive programs," for example, have been accused of duplicating services already available in a community. Such duplication often occurs because of a lack of links between various elements in the program. As programs become more complex, arrangements and differences in outcome may accrue, depending upon the ordering of the individual's various engagements with elements of the program. To illustrate: Some children may be exposed to a program designed to stimulate reading, both in school and in a neighborhood community center. Are the effects of these two programs additive? Does the individual gain as much from each program as he would have had he not been exposed to the other? A model which takes into consideration the complex question of possible interaction of the program's elements is required.

It is even possible that interacting elements of a program may counteract each other. For example, prior to the urban redevelopment of an area, a community-relations program may be initiated in order to obtain the cooperation of community members. At the same time, the stresses connected with urban relocation may necessitate the immediate establishment of the housing relocation office. The community-relations program may increase the identity of neighborhood residents with each other and with their neighborhood, but the very visible relocation office is there to move them out.

The Epidemiological Model. The epidemiological approach of public-health researchers is useful in developing impact models (Mac-Mahon, *et al.,* 1960). Public-health officials quite often conceptualize causal phenomena into three domains—host, agent, and environment—and hold that intervention in any of these domains will result in a modification. They would argue, for example, that malaria can be reduced by eradicating the mosquito that spreads the germ, the germ itself, or the swamps in which the mosquitoes live. Thus, a fly swatter, a vaccination, or putting oil on swampy ponds are alternative strategies of intervention. The epidemiological model is a way of stating a multicausal hypothesis, and it is presented here as an illustration of the way such causal notions may be organized for intervention programs.

There are other approaches as well, such as seeking out the successive steps in a process, illustrated by Becker (1955) in his discussion of how one becomes a marijuana user. He argues that a variety of successive actions have to occur: The individual has to have access to marijuana. He has to smoke it. His reaction to the smoking has to be gratifying to him. Finally, he has to have some assurance that his reaction will not eventuate some undesirable subsequent result.

Curvilinear Relationships. Causal relationships need not always be linear. In some areas it may rarely be the case that successive increases or decreases in a particular phenomenon have the same effect. For example, most cardiac specialists maintain that weight is related to cardiac disease and that diet and exercise to reduce weight will reduce the likelihood that an individual will suffer cardiac failure. Certainly though, there is a point where insufficient food or overexercise will have undesirable consequences.

In general, social scientists have not paid enough attention to the specification of curvilinear relationships, and most statements are of a linear sort. This is because of the added complexity of thinking in non-linear terms and the lack of adequate statistical methods of quantitative analysis. Nevertheless, in the specification of impact models, presumptions of linearity need to be made explicit and thought must be given to whether the presumption can be made workable. (Curvilinear relationships will be discussed again later in this chapter, when we describe the selection of a target population.)

Sources of Hypotheses

Ideally, the hypotheses embodied in impact models should stem from one of two sources, either from experimental studies that permit causal inferences or from logically developed theories. In actuality, causal studies and logically developed theories of social behavior and social processes are scarce. Most impact models are derived either from clinical impressions or from statistical associations. Each of these four sources requires some elaboration.

Causal Studies. Impact models which link interventions to cause and outcome are an integration or synthesis of independent experimental studies. We may know from the laboratory, for example, that penicillin increases the number of white blood cells. We might also know, from other studies, that an increase in white blood cells causes a reduction of a certain infectious bacteria. An impact model can then be developed, by linking the two findings, which states that the provision of penicillin leads to an increase in white blood cells, which leads to a reduction in certain infectious germs.

In certain areas of psychology, enough laboratory studies have been done so that impact models are to some degree based upon causal analysis. For the most part, however, the difficulties of manipulation and the problems of cost and measurement have minimized the number of experimental studies in social research. Impact models based on experimental studies are therefore rare in social-policy research.

Logical Theories. In many fields of science, great emphasis is placed upon the development of formal or logical theories in which statements explaining a process are linked to each other by a system of logic (Costner, 1964). There is considerable formal theory building in the social sciences, and interest in their development has been stimulated by the availability of computers and the opportunity to use them in constructing the logical systems. For the most part, however, there is still little use of formal theoretical ideas in impact models, because of the nature of the problems typically assessed by theorists.

Clinical Impressions. Ideas for impact models often come from the experience of individuals who have dealt with a particular condition or behavior. In almost every field of practice—medicine, social work, rehabilitation, and so forth—practitioners are constantly making judgments about their success and failure and about the utility of one type of intervention in comparison with another. The practitioner often systematically records the results of his interventions, and thus has "evidence" about their utility. Since he does not conduct a formal experiment, however, he is essentially making a prediction which can be tested on an experimental basis.

The experience of practitioners is a valuable source for the development of impact models. As we have noted, however, explicit statements of exactly what is to happen are difficult to develop. It may be impossible to duplicate the therapeutic intervention in a particular case because the practitioner's description of what took place was unclear or imprecise. One consequence of the engagement of social-policy researchers in program development is that they help to create a climate in which explication becomes an important responsibility of the practitioner and thus the utility of clinical experience increased.

Predictive Studies. Although there is a paucity of experimental studies, the growth of the social and psychological sciences has brought about an accumulation of predictive findings. That is, attention to various social problems has yielded extensive statements about the probability that one variable is associated with another. For example, studies have suggested that there are links between various facets of the adolescent's social situation and his criminal behavior. In many instances, association between variables shown by the raw empirical data has been refined, either by sophisticated statistical analysis or by a synthesis of various studies, into what is called a "middle-range theory" (Merton, 1966).

Statistical analysis may be employed to demonstrate the continued presence of the association when other conditions presumed to be causal conditions have been removed. It also may be undertaken to introduce new variables which strengthen the argument that there is a link between the variables originally under study (Lazarsfeld, 1955). As we have seen, the hypotheses that come out of the clinical impressions of practitioners are a special type of predictive study, the difference being the degree of precision and systemization of the work.

Because experimental results and formal theories are scarce, predictive research is important to program development. The policy maker operates, for the most part, on the basis of hypotheses derived from predictive analyses. He is almost always putting together two or more sets of correlational findings and then making presumptions that modifications of one factor will produce changes in another. We know, of course, that correlations may not indicate cause or yield the best intervention program. Yet, there is no choice but to depend on correlations, given the current state of knowledge in the social sciences.

Manipulability, and the Feasibility of Intervention

Impact models are based on the presumption that the variables which constitute the phenomenon being modified are open to manipulation. Variables associated with either the causal or outcome variables of a program, however, are often "selection" rather than "contextual" variables. This means that the phenomena exist because individuals or aspects of the environment were sorted out in a particular manner at a prior point in time. Manipulability, therefore, is precluded. This apparently is partly the case in the area of educational achievement. Much of the variance in the high-school performance of students, for example, is evidently not a function of what happens to them in high school; it is due to the influence of their family and their early social environment (Sewell, 1966). If the extent of poor performance in high school leads to a decision by policy makers to design programs to remedy the situation, therefore, the intervention may have to take place when the students are younger. The children now of high-school age would be sacrificed. The focus of a program clearly needs to be on measures which are manipulable at some point in time, and the time must be known.

In developing a program one must avoid selecting variables whose manipulability is remote. This may be so because of technical limitations, because of the ideological values and imperatives of community life, or because of the risk of undesired side-effects. For example, in a program developed to reduce air pollution, certain variables, such as the amount of fumes given off by automobiles, would be found to be manipulable, and others such as the reduction of waste from certain industrial operations, would be found not to be manipulable because of a lack of technical knowledge. In this case, technology dictates a focus on one set of variables rather than on another. Ideological and political imperatives can be illustrated by another problem. Social class has been found to be correlated with mental illness, but a revolutionary change in our economic structure is hardly the intervention sought by the policy maker. The social-policy researcher must therefore identify the variables open to manipulation. The undesirable side-effects can be illustrated by the use of telephone tapping to identify certain criminals, such as bookmakers. But telephone tapping would of necessity include listening in on the innocent as well as the guilty, an invasion of privacy which militates against this kind of intervention.

It is crucial that the policy researcher be sensitive to the need for manipulability. The ability of the social-policy researcher to conceptualize predictive studies into programs which meet the criterion of manipulability is one distinction which can be made between the policy researcher and his academic peer.

The Selection of Target Populations

Another important decision in program development is the selection of a target population. Social-policy decisions are normally made with a view to the needs of various groups within the community. Prediction thus requires that the data be gathered from a particular perspective. For example, decisions regarding programs to reduce illiteracy may be based on information about the prevalence of literacy in the population. Information is then sought about how the rate varies in different groups or, to use predictive terms, about the characteristics that are associated with illiteracy. There is interplay, as should be clear, between the selection of the target population and the development of the impact model; consequently, the choice of the target population is a strategic decision. The character of programs may be sharply shifted if it is found that the characteristics of the target population are not what they were originally thought to be.

IDEOLOGICAL CONSIDERATIONS

Decisions about target populations typically involve ideological as well as pragmatic considerations. Among policy makers there are continual ideological debates, and the policy researcher must be aware of the arguments that are relevant to his particular area of program development. Some of the issues reflect basic philosophical values about social change in a democratic society. One debate, for example, that explicitly or implicitly is involved in program development in the fields of health, welfare, and education revolves around whether the focus should be on residual programs or on institutional programs.

Residual vs. Institutional Programs. Residual programs "pick up the pieces," so to speak, and institutional programs are broad community-wide efforts that will have a direct and indirect effect on the target group. Welfare payments are commonly viewed as a residual mechanism, providing people with the wherewithal to subsist. Encouraging the opening of new factories in the community on the other hand, would be regarded as an institutional program. The argument for the latter program is that, in addition to perhaps providing a few jobs for the indigent, it will improve occupational opportunities for the entire community and the benefits will filter down to the unemployed on government support. Improved transportation in the community, rather than special bus fares for the poor, would be an institutional, rather than a residual, expenditure.

The Relation of the Target Population to the Impact Model. A second underlying philosophical issue is whether one seeks to modify the target population so that its members may participate in programs and services not formerly enjoyed, or whether one modifies programs and services to make them more consistent with the behavior and style of life of the target population. The decision is rarely easy. In the provision of health services, for instance, it is argued that if the economically disadvantaged are taught to communicate better with professional people and to expect "middle-class medicine," this would solve their medical problems and eliminate the need for many special clinics and programs. Another solution also advocated is to make medical care available on a basis which is consistent with the orientation and expectations of the lower socioeconomic groups. The area of public health provides good illustrations, because some existing programs are based on one point of view and some on the other.

In considering the selection of the target population, the social-policy researcher should be aware that it is often desirable to distinguish between the population that is going to be directly subjected to intervention and the population that requires attention. This depends on the impact model. Suppose the problem is to increase the income of the unemployed. Rather than provide increased welfare payments, let us say, for the unemployed (the population that requires attention), the government might decide to intervene with employers, permitting special income-tax deductions for those who hire workers with a long history of unemployment. To predict the effect of such intervention, the social-policy researcher would have to assess, either from past studies or after the collection of new data, the relationship between economic dispensations and employment, a task surely as important as predicting the composition of the target population, unemployed workers, from their social and psychological characteristics.

Likewise, because of the relationship between the way programs are organized and their acceptance and utilization by target populations, prediction studies have to account for the way a program is organized and why it should be accepted. The health field again provides a useful illustration. Correlational studies suggest that lack of prenatal care, particularly during the last months of pregnancy, is related to subsequent health problems for the mother and for the new baby, among them, a higher likelihood of mental retardation of the child. The target population in this instance is partially identifiable. It includes unmarried mothers, particularly in low-income areas. The solution advocated is often simplistic; that is, to increase the available medical facilities in low-income areas which have large populations of young women. It does not necessarily follow that the increase would lead to the increased use of the medical services by unmarried mothers, however.

In some ways, the distinction between the two predictive tasks, the development of an impact model and the selection of a target population, is artificial. The impact model must include within it a set of hypotheses about the plausibility of one event leading to another event. Such sets rest upon predictions about the characteristics of the target population in relation to the intervention.

PRAGMATIC CONSIDERATIONS

There are different ways of viewing the prediction procedure in relation to the target population. Some of our comments are applicable to the impact model as well. In the selection of the target population, the object is to identify the group which has the most need for the program or which is most likely to benefit from the use of the resources which are to be made available. Sometimes the choice rests on balancing need against the likelihood of benefit.

Measuring the Variables Which Predict the Target Population. The variables used in selecting the target population must be readily measurable. For example, a predictive study might suggest that nonvirginity among females is an excellent predictor of the likelihood of becoming an unmarried mother. However, programs designed to reduce illegitimacy cannot make use of such information without considerable modification in what community members know about each other. Thus the criterion of age may be used, even though its correlation with the likelihood of becoming an unmarried mother may be lower. Rather than a measure that is in and of itself a much more robust predictor, age (along with sex), becomes the definer of the target population.

Individual Prediction. Predictive studies are directed at the question of how to "win the most bets" in estimating variations in a particular type of behavior or community condition. One is not gambling, however, against a real opponent; the foe is chance. Predictive studies begin with the assumption that, in the absence of knowledge of variables correlated with the phenomenon under examination, the distribution of the behavior itself is the most valuable bit of knowledge. This is particularly true of prediction on an individual, case-by-case basis (Horst, 1941). Individual prediction is useful, for instance, in selecting from among mental patients the target population for a long-term educational program. In the absence of other information, if one discovers that in the past 70 per cent of all mental patients remained out of the hospital for at least a year after discharge, the best guess about each patient is that he is going to remain out of the hospital for this period.

One simple way of determining the utility of a variable in individual prediction is to calculate the improved accuracy of the prediction when more variables are added. If 70 per cent of a hospital's population will be out of the hospital for a year after discharge, but only 20 per cent of those 45 and over, this bit of information makes possible differential and more efficient predictions about individual patients. The second variable, age, permits the reduction of the number of errors by 40 per cent. If all a wise gambler knew was that 700 former patients out of 1,000 remained in the community for a year, and he made a bet on each one, he would bet that all the patients would remain that long in the community and would lose 300 of his 1,000 bets. If he also knew the age of the patient and the relationship between age and remaining in the community, he would bet that all patients under 45 would remain in the community a year, and that all those 45 and over would return sooner to the hospital. He would lose 140 bets in the under-45 group and 40 bets in the over-45 group—a total of 180 in 1,000. His prediction errors (lost bets) would be reduced from 300 to 180, a difference of 120 and a reduction of 40 per cent.

TABLE 4.1

Age and Community Tenure of 1,000 Patients

	Age		
	Under 45	45 and Over	Total
Remain in Community	660	40	700
Do not Remain in Community	140	160	300
Total	800	200	1,000

Group Prediction. The other type of prediction undertaken is group prediction. Here the gambler is not necessarily concerned with the individual case, but with the characteristics of the group. He examines either changes in proportions that occur when more information is available, or the behavior of the dependent variable when one or more predictive variables are taken into account. These alternatives are illustrated by Tables 4.2 and 4.3 below.

The first table, showing the cross-classification of variables, and the second, called a "scatter-gram," both provide opportunities for prediction. While eye color does not permit better individual predictions (i.e.,

TABLE 4.2

Association between Eye Color and Marital Status

	Married	*Single*
Green	70%	30%
Blue	60%	40%
Brown	50%	50%

regardless of eye color, most persons are married), they do allow for statements of probability on a group basis. According to the tables, green-eyed persons are most likely to be married, and poorly educated persons are most likely to have low incomes.

Undertaking Predictive Studies. A variety of computational statistics are used in deriving estimates of the extent of predictability. For many purposes, including some very practical ones, it makes no difference what predictor variables are in a study, as long as they have predictive power. The warden of a prison might be willing to use color of hair, shape of head, or length of thumb to decide who should be paroled—if these were strongly associated with successful tenure in a community.

The main thrust of a prediction study is to maximize predictability. The researcher works toward finding a small number of predictors which

TABLE 4.3

Correlation between Annual Income
and Grades Completed in School

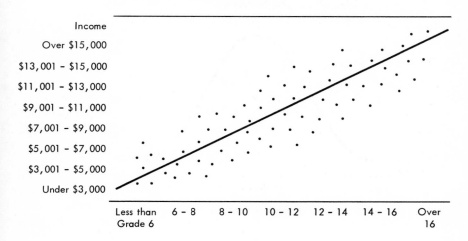

minimize the number of errors, and he uses previous empirical research, theoretical notions, and the most sophisticated and sensitive statistical approach. There is a literature on the appropriate methodology for making predictive studies (Edward, 1957), and ongoing work continues to provide more sophisticated means of undertaking studies. The thinking involved, however, is already sufficient for social-policy research purposes.

Predictive analysis often involves exceedingly complex statistical techniques (Ezekiel and Fox, 1959). Even the most basic types of correlational analysis require extensive calculations, now made much easier, of course, by computers. As one moves, however, from linear to curvilinear approaches to prediction, the statistical operations require greater sophistication. Although social researchers customarily use linear predictive models—that is, they try to fit a straight line to the data—many events, as we observed earlier, are better described by curves. A researcher interested in predicting what the target population for a delinquency program should be might find that nondelinquent high-school students include those with few or no absences as well as those with a large number of absences. The target population, therefore, should consist of students with a moderate number of absences. This point is illustrated in Table 4.4.

It is unrealistic to assume that all social-policy researchers are highly qualified statistical analysts, for this is not so among social-science researchers in general. They often require consultants who are skilled in the necessary techniques. However, the social-policy researcher should be

TABLE 4.4

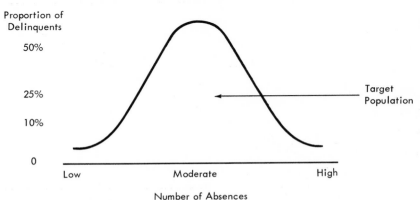

Correlation between Absences from
High School and Delinquency

reasonably knowledgeable about the conclusions and inferences that those engaged in program development can draw from prediction analyses.

Concluding Comment

The tasks of developing an impact model and identifying the target population are ones in which the social researcher can play a vital role. Local and even national programs are frequently carried out without adequate specification of the impact model or the target population. Much of the criticism of social-service programs stems from this failure.

In applying himself to these two basic tasks, the social-policy researcher must, at one and the same time, become familiar with the practices that are being envisaged in the proposed program or that have been used elsewhere, and he must maintain a questioning, somewhat cynical posture toward contemplated efforts. It is simply too easy for him to become so caught up in the design of programs that he fails to insist upon the specificity that good program development requires.

Chapter 5

EVALUATION

It is poor social policy to plan and execute programs, certainly innovative ones, without provision for their evaluation. It is in the evaluation process that the policy maker reasserts his participation in the planning, development, and carrying out of policy. However, the possibility of undertaking a useful evaluation of a program of prevention, amelioration, or rehabilitation rests upon how well the antecedent aspects of program development were worked out.

Evaluation is usually worthless if there has not been adequate planning of a well-explicated program. Inadequacies in planning, as well as in execution severely limit the possibilities of evaluation. Even today, persons who work on planning and on program development, who agree on an abstract level with the necessity for evaluation, are often placed in a position where their activities are less than completely undertaken, virtually eliminating the possibility of evaluation. Times have changed remarkably, however, and it is becoming difficult for practitioners and policy makers to defend the omission of evaluation, especially at the federal level. Congress, as well as key individuals in the various executive departments, are insisting upon adequate evaluation of their own operations and of the large contracts and demonstration programs that they administer (Freeman and Sherwood, 1965). The demand for evidence of usefulness undoubtedly will increase further.

The Tasks in Evaluation

The evaluation process should include two activities. The first is essentially a procedure for controlling quantity and quality. Mechanisms for determining whether the actual conduct of programs is consistent with the intervention strategy outlined in the development of the program have to be set up. In other words, is the designated target population the one that is receiving the services? Are the services that were to be provided the ones that are actually being provided? This assessment of the execution of the program is, for the most part, a descriptive task.

The research task which has a causal character is the assessment of the impact of the program. Obviously, many programs can be provided as stipulated, and to the specified target populations, and yet have no impact. The policy maker is interested in efficacy of the program, that is, the extent to which it works. He is also concerned with its cost. Unless he knows something about the cost of a benefit provided by a program, he will have a very limited basis for deciding whether that program should be continued and expanded. Moreover, he will have insufficient information on which to compare the many programs that he must often choose among them (U.S. Department of Health, Education, and Welfare, 1968).

The evaluation process is the aspect of social-policy development in which planners and program persons are most dependent upon social researchers. The other phases of policy development are occasionally undertaken entirely without research personnel, but the technicalities of evaluation and the conduct of evaluation assessments require the skills and the orientation of the researcher. It is this dependence upon social researchers for the evaluation operation that has led to the recognition that a research unit is needed within a policy-making organization or that, at minimum, there must be continuing relationships with social investigators who are skilled in evaluation research.

THE ASSESSMENT OF THE EXECUTION OF A PROGRAM

As we have noted, one element in the evaluation process is the assessment of whether or not the action program has conformed to the procedures outlined in its design. First, it is important to know whether the program has been directed at the appropriate target population or at the specified target area. Second, it is necessary to gauge whether or not the various practices and remedial efforts were undertaken as specified in the program design or, at least, whether or not they were derived from the principles explicated in that design (Suchman, 1967).

The assessment of program implementation is an administrative task in that it is a mechanism by which the policy maker is able to ascertain whether persons are doing what they are supposed to do. Clearly, the effectiveness of the policy-making organization depends upon whether operating personnel are conforming with the mandates of policy-making personnel. If not, the policy-making role will atrophy. Program assessment is not simply an administrative matter, however. As we have indicated, the development of policy is a dynamic process wherein the policy maker constantly modifies, expands, and shifts the activities under his purview. Unless he knows what is going on, it is difficult to contemplate changes or to project future developments.

Persons without experience in preventive, remedial, and rehabilitative efforts, we repeat, may not be aware of the discrepancies between what policy makers say should be done and what is actually done. The phenomenon of dissonance between program specifications and their actual conduct, however, is usually not a consequence of charlatanism or corruption. It is related to the inadequate supervision of practitioners and to limitations in resources. Even in the presence of adequate personnel and other resources, the day-to-day pressures of work may limit the practitioner's ability to judge how well his program conforms to the mandates set forth when the program was developed. In addition, in many instances the practitioner finds it difficult to effectuate principles which have been left at too conceptual a level by the policy maker.

The Importance of Specifying the Target Population. It also bears repeating that the assessment of the implementation of a program requires the explicit and detailed specification of the target population. The specification of the target population may be limited by inadequate work during the program's development, or, it may be left purposely vague in order to allow for flexibility in the commitment of resources. For example, during the planning phase there may be considerable evidence of serious malnutrition among young children. The identification of the target population may be limited to specifying some geopolitical boundaries for the program; and no specific entrance requirements may be proposed for the program's participants in terms of degree and type of malnutrition. The lack of specificity may occur for a number of reasons: the people involved in the program may have varying ideas about how to measure malnutrition; or they may be unsure of the cooperation of persons in the target area and do not want to be specific about the potential target population. The fear of underutilization of programs is a real one for the persons who run them.

There also may be pragmatic difficulties in focusing services on specific target populations. Part of this problem is a moral one. Returning to our example, even if the specification of the target population is quite exact and the program to alleviate malnutrition were limited to persons with specific height-weight imbalances or other visible symptoms, what happens if individuals who are not so severely undernourished request services? In many cases, the practitioners involved in the program are reluctant or unwilling to turn them away. To take another example, social-activity programs may be set up for persons over 65. What happens if a person in his early sixties, and in obvious need of such services, appears at the door?

Another part of the problem of confining programs to specified target populations is political and administrative. Groups are often excluded from the target population because of their lesser need for the program or because there are other services available to them. These groups may use a variety of pressures to gain entrance to a program despite their stated ineligibility. They may enlist the aid of elected officials. Public programs cannot be unresponsive to requests from individuals with political influence, and it would be unrealistic to deny the need of their support for activities in health, education, and welfare.

Related to the problem of influence and the occasional use of undesirable means to sidestep the criteria for entrance into a program is the administrative difficulty of enforcing some criteria. Practitioners and administrators in many programs argue forcibly that the costs and problems involved in processing individuals in terms of particular criteria are not worth it. The simplest way around the problem often is to ignore the criteria imposed during planning and program development. An excellent dental clinic program for young children run by a local public health program, for example, has a theoretical requirement that its services are for low-income families only, and a specified scale of income in relation to family size has been established (Lambert and Freeman, 1967). Using the criterion, however, would require some sort of financial investigation of the families, a difficult and distasteful procedure. In consequence, the mere application for treatment is accepted as evidence of financial need and, except in extremely obvious cases of ineligibility, no effort is made to restrict the clientele in terms of the financial requirement.

The social-policy researcher need not take a stand with regard to the restriction of services; his task is to inform the personnel responsible for the program's development and execution of the actual state of affairs. There are times when new information results in a redefinition of the target population which legitimizes the utilization of a program by persons who were formerly considered inappropriate. The important point to be made is that the failure to acknowledge discrepancies between the stated and the actual utilization of services destroys the likelihood of rational planning in the future as well as any effective evaluation of the efficacy of an existing program.

Estimating the Target Population. Even when all the characteristics of the target population are specified during the program's development and execution, another task remains. Estimating the extent to which the program is being directed at the group identified as the target population requires research. If the characteristics are specified, some means of tallying the actual population in the program is usually the simplest solution. Many programs have record systems that include measures of the variables or characteristics which describe the target population. Even the simplest record system, however, entails at least three important considerations.

The first consideration is a pragmatic one: the operations of programs cannot become subservient to the data-collection process. Developing a format for data collection often requires considerable creativity. The format must contain a procedure for measuring the target population which is not time-consuming, which does not overly involve staff who are needed for other tasks, and which can be analyzed and reported on with despatch. Second, the development of procedures for estimating the target population often requires the development of reliable and valid measures that were not considered when the program was evolved. Unless the instrumentation is craftsmanlike, there is no point to the procedure. Third, it must be ascertained that the actual collection of the data does not deteriorate. The demands on the program's personnel to do other things must not turn the process into a superficial, ritualistic one. Constant surveillance of the operation is required for this reason, and because practitioners may come to realize that they are not hitting the target population. Without surveillance, they may circumvent the criteria by "fitting the cases in" where they think they are needed.

The development and maintenance of records and statistics may involve the researcher with operating staff, who may regard him as part of management or, even worse, a spy. Frequently, practitioners want to know why the information is going to be gathered, who is going to have access to it, and what is going to be done with it. The social researcher who wants to develop means of examining the correspondence between the people who receive a service and those for whom the service is intended may find himself in the position of an interpreter of policy to the practitioner.

A mere examination of the recipients of service, however, often proves to be insufficient, particularly when the characteristics of the target population have not been fully explicated. Even when they have been, it is important to understand something about the extent to which the needs of the population are being met. This involves a comparative analysis between treated and untreated persons.

Previously, we used the example of a program to reduce malnutrition in a community to illustrate some of the problems of defining a target population. Let us say that the mandate is to provide a food supplement to severely malnourished children in a particular neighborhood. How might one go about examining whether the appropriate target population had been reached? One approach that certainly would be used would be to collect a variety of measures of malnutrition, such as deficiencies in height and weight or medical examinations of the persons who were receiving the food supplement. The researcher would want to know, of course, if individuals without symptoms of malnutrition were also receiving the supplement.

A second approach that commends itself is to select a representative sample of neighborhood children. There should be less malnourishment in the sample than in the group that is part of the program; if not, the appropriateness of the program should be questioned.

The cost of such comparative information to estimate the extent to which the commitment to the target population was realized is often prohibitive, however. As we have observed earlier, there is utility to using secondary or already-collected data whenever possible. The data obtained from the recipients of service, economical because the recipients constitute in part at least a captive audience, may be compared with existing norms or other available profiles. This is one of the justifications of a careful examination of available data during the planning period. Such information not only helps in planning and developing the program, but also provides a backdrop for understanding the degree of service rendered to the target population.

The Importance of Examining Conformity to the Impact Model. It is often difficult to examine whether a program has been undertaken according to the specifications outlined during its development. Practitioners may have autonomy, or they may have a dual commitment, and privacy and dignity are required in relationships with recipients of services. Programs that are mechanical rarely face this problem, but most activities in health, education, and welfare involve a relationship between the practitioner and the client. The professional practitioner, particularly, is prepared to work in a relatively independent and unsupervised way, and one is reluctant to delve too deeply into what he actually does on the job.

The problem of conformity is a severe one in virtually every field, and there are numerous anecdotes about the difficulties of making certain that a program is being carried out as it is supposed to be. Certain preventive programs to detect cancer, for example, specify a series of body sites that are to be examined, but there is evidence that even some well-qualified internists find rectal examinations extremely distasteful and either avoid them or make them only superficially.

Probably the chief difficulty, however, is in the communication to the practitioner of the actual steps to be undertaken. In many types of programs, the temperament and personality of the practitioner or his client, or the environment in which the program is undertaken intrude on efforts at uniformity. A common program in delinquency prevention, for example, involves the use of detached-workers who develop relationships with adolescents and adolescent gangs on the streets, working closely with them to modify their values and norms and to redirect their activities toward lawful behavior. Many of these programs recruit their detached workers from schools of social work. The workers therefore have a somewhat common educational background as well as specific direction and supervision, and it might be presumed that they would perform equally. This is hardly the case, however, as Kantor and Bennett (1968) have indicated. The style of the workers varies, and there is no single type. Some maintain a "professional orientation," trying to be objective and constantly testing out new approaches. Other are "moralists" who are less sensitive to goals and techniques but more sensitive to the needs of the boys. Some are primarily interested in the extent to which they can "get in" with the boys; others, with the degree to which they are capable of manipulating the gang.

It is presumed too freely that common training and common apprenticeship minimizes differences between professionals. Minimization of differences in styles of work is difficult when interpersonal skills are involved (as they usually are) and when a variety of environmental situations are endemic to the program. Surgeons from the same medical and residency programs, working in hospitals, are probably more alike in their behavior than general practitioners seeing patients in their homes. Variability need not always be a deficiency, but the policy group is clearly entitled to know what is going on.

Examining Programs. The examination of operating programs is, to a large extent, *field work*—that is, direct observation of what is taking place. The idea of field work in the social sciences is based upon the view that neither the secondary reports of participants nor an evaluation of the outcome of social relationships and experiences provides sufficient evidence that a particular process occurred the way it was assumed it would (Bruyn, 1966; Habenstein, 1969). The field approach, then, is an effort to report the actual interactions and social processes that occur among individuals related to each other interpersonally.

Field studies are a common part of the spectrum of research activities undertaken in anthropology and sociology. Studies have been made of a variety of groups and communities, as well as on more microscopic situations such as educational programs and industrial corporations (Becker et al., 1961). In some of these studies, the researcher actually becomes a participant or semi-participant so that he can describe what goes on without the added input of an investigator. In others, he remains identified as an outsider; however, it is generally thought that he soon ceases to be a novelty and that the persons involved soon behave pretty much as usual (Whyte, 1943). Examining what goes on in operating programs ordinarily does not involve the full-blown use of field-study methods, however. The observer is most concerned with the practices that supposedly are to be carried out as specified in the impact model.

There are several criticisms of the use of field studies in the evaluation of social-policy research. The two of importance to us here have to do with the variability of observations made by observers with different training and characteristics, and with the limitations of the accuracy of reporting. While it is foolhardy to think that many of the apparent variations in operating programs can be accounted for in this way, it is only fair to say that the problem of understanding what takes place may indeed be related to the variability of the observers as well as to the variability of the practitioners.

There is little reason to assume consistency in what observers see, and especially in what they report. There are many methods of recording observations, and investigators continually try to develop mechanisms for producing greater consistency and reliability. When the series of operations to be observed can be specified very precisely, it is possible to use a checklist. This approach probably results in more consistent observations. In other cases, however, the purpose of assessing an operating program is to find out what the practitioners are actually doing in programs which have only a vague impact model. The method usually employed in these instances is to record the process: That is, the observer attempts, after a period of observation, to put down as closely as possible the actual interactions and social processes observed. There are many intermediate variants between checklist completion and process recording. Most investigating teams rely on some combination of training and supervision of the observers in order to assure modicum of reliability.

The development of a design for observing what goes on involves the investigator in a number of technical decisions. Naturally, it is not possible for him to observe what goes on all of the time among all of the practitioners engaged in a program. It is usually necessary for him to decide upon sample periods during which observations are made. He should try to assure himself that these sample periods are representative of the total operation of the program. In many cases, however, it is necessary to undertake the observation procedures at a more superficial level than is desired. Cost, the need to remain inconspicuous, and the difficulty of analyzing the data (a technical problem which will be discussed later) frequently limit this type of assessment. Nevertheless, observation is a necessary part of any assessment. Most social investigators, as Suchman (1967) indicates, know that the impact of a program is not proved merely because something is done in the way the professionals think it should be done. When action is not undertaken according to specification or in professionally astute ways, then there is certainly reason to question the efficacy of the program.

There are, of course, situations in which observations of actual events are impossible. We have already alluded to the problems of privacy and the possibility that observation will interfere with the ongoing program, and it is worth noting again that observation is expensive. When it is impossible to make direct observations, social investigators are forced to turn to the practitioners, their supervisors, or to the recipients of the service for reports of what went on. Although there are limitations to the use of secondhand information of this type, it is often the only information about the interactional and interpersonal situation that can be obtained. Different schemes have been developed to try to increase the usefulness of secondary reports. Frequently, the same observations are obtained from two or more informants, and consistency in their reports is regarded as evidence of their accuracy.

Secondary reporting procedures may place considerable strain upon the informants. Supervisors who are called upon to verify aspects of an operating program may feel a professional identification with and a loyalty to persons on their staff. They may themselves be implicated in unanticipated and unplanned departures from the program as specified in the impact model. In most programs certainly, more knowledge than exists is required of what goes on.

The quality-control function, that is, obtaining data on the execution of programs, is only one purpose of evaluation research. If programs are going to be expanded to different locations or situations, and if a large number of individuals are going to be used as agents of social change, it is necessary to be able to tell practitioners with some clarity and specificity what they are supposed to do. Only if the experimental programs or the programs in existence are codified can we begin to have a mechanism, and the necessary empirical information, with which to ensure that the programs can be approximated in other situations. More important, if there is an experimental evaluation of a particular impact model without an evaluation of the actual conduct of the program, an efficacious and socially useful strategy may be tossed aside. Certainly there are cases where interventions have been deemed ineffectual when in fact they never occurred.

THE ASSESSMENT OF IMPORT

Earlier, in discussing the tasks involved in developing social programs, the notion of experimental evaluations was commented upon in perhaps somewhat more detail than the other tasks discussed. The reason for this is the authors' belief that people still need to be persuaded of the need for experimental evaluations. Experimental evaluations constitute the common means by which a causal link between an input and an outcome can be demonstrated. There are cases in which it is possible to unravel the causal links among phenomena without undertaking experiments, usually because it is safe to assume a definite time sequence. For example, if one finds a relationship between the use of alcohol and automobile accidents, and it is possible to rule out other contaminating determinants, it would be pretty safe to assume that drinking causes accidents, and not the converse. There are a number of analysts who have approached cause statistically, through sophisticated models or complex statistical control of determinants, taking into account the time sequence or using general causal models (Duncan, 1966; Blalock, 1964). In general, however, in social-policy research we are almost always dependent on experimental investigations. The objective in experimental evaluations is to be able to say definitively that a particular intervention has led to a particular change which results in a phenomenon that would not have occurred otherwise. As we have noted, experimental evaluations require control groups, in their absence it is not possible to assure that the only substantial difference is the exposure of the experimental group to the intervention program.

The Design of Evaluation Studies. Designs of experimental evaluations are a compromise between the specified rules and models of the experimental method, on the one hand, and what can be done ethically and pragmatically, given the realities of the situation in which the intervention has taken place, on the other. Some technical details of the conduct of experiments will be considered in the next chapter; here, it should be noted that while clean experiments, like those conducted in a laboratory, are virtually impossible, there are more opportunities for experimental evaluations than might be expected.

Usually, two compromises are made in evaluation experiments that are not always necessary in the laboratory. The first stems from the moral and ethical problems involved in having experimental groups and groups receiving no treatment. In many evaluation studies, rather than using a control group which receives either no treatment or a placebo, the impact of a program is compared with that of a commonplace or traditional situation, or the impact of a set of programs is assessed by comparing programs in the set to each other. For example, many would think it unethical to deny *all* treatment to a randomly selected control group of mental patients. Yet, if the aim is to evaluate the impact of a new mode of therapy, most people would think it entirely legitimate to have a control group from among those who are receiving the usual, ordinary types of treatment and then to compare their improvement with that of the experimental group.

The second compromise has to do with the selection of subjects for the experimental and control groups. In most laboratory situations, subjects are randomly assigned; in evaluation studies, there are many tactical reasons why this cannot entirely be done. It may be administratively unfeasible in certain situations. For example, the intention may be to evaluate the impact of a reading program using a teaching machine on the delinquent behavior of adolescents, but the teaching machines may be usable only in regular classrooms. The investigator cannot randomize boys for this program. He must employ randomization by classes, introducing possibly dissimilar groups, and the subsequent analysis of the data will have to take into account the potential statistical variations among these different groups. While the computer makes it possible to use sophisticated statistical procedures to reduce selection differences among groups (a more extended discussion of this matter will follow in a subsequent chapter), the limitation on randomization is nevertheless an important one in the experimental evaluation of this reading program.

A word should be said about the problem of understanding causal sequences once they are uncovered by an evaluation study. As we indicated in our discussion of the role of evaluation in the development of social policy, merely knowing that something works is usually insufficient. One is also concerned with understanding why it works. Knowing why something works helps to reduce some of the psychic anxiety that man seems to have when he does not understand what is going on; moreover, an understanding of the causal process may permit a simpler and even more efficacious program to be developed. The basis for understanding a causal sequence is the impact model. Programs do not develop out of thin air. They are the consequence either of theoretical notions or of empirical data which suggest correlations between variables or phenomena. Usually, as part of program development and in the construction of the impact model, some kind of conceptual statement is offered as a potential explanation of the linkages. When the linkages are found to hold experimentally, one may return to that statement as a point of departure for understanding the causal process.

Efficacy and Efficiency. In examining results of programs, particularly by means of experimental evaluation, the tendency is to focus on the efficacy of the approach. By *efficacy,* we mean that the input changed the target group or environment in the direction expected, and that such a change would occur again if the experiment were repeated. In other words, a judgment is made that the experimental group has improved significantly more than its almost-mirror image, the control group.

Efficiency refers to *the improvement in terms of some measure of unit cost.* An example should make the point obvious. One children's program may cost $10 per subject but change only 10 out of 100 children. The cost of service per child is $10, but the cost per case of efficient service is $100. Another program that costs $20 per child but desirably affects 50 children has a cost per case of efficient service of only $40. It may well be that a program which seems to be the most expensive is the most economical from the standpoint of benefits derived.

Efficacy and efficiency are related concepts. When two competing programs are being compared, the question of which is more efficacious can be answered in terms of the relative difference between what happens in one program as opposed to what happens in another. For example, a special summer program, emphasizing intellectual skills, may be developed for young children. The control group may be in an ordinary nursery school. The evaluation may show no significant differences between the results of the programs—the conclusion would be that the innovative program had no special impact.

If both appear to be equally advantageous, however, then the concept of efficiency becomes crucial. Efficiency is virtually synonymous with the notion of cost-benefit, but it is a somewhat broader term because there is no need, and in fact it might be undesirable, to calculate all outcomes in terms of dollars. As we observed in our earlier discussion of descriptive data, however, money is frequently used. Results can be reported in a form which policy makers and lay community leaders can grasp. Second, to use cost permits a comparison of studies in different programmatic areas—and policy makers, particularly broad-gauge ones, have to make choices not only between programs in the same areas but between programs in different areas. Finally, since most social programs require money, expressions in dollars permit us to gain some idea of the cost of a broad-scale program.

Concern with the cost and benefits of programs, continues to increase particularly of public programs (see Kalen, 1969 for a discussion of program budgeting and cost effectiveness). It is not merely a natural limitation of resources that has created a consciousness of the necessity for a cost–benefit approach. The newer broad programs which attempt to create massive modifications in the social structure of communities require extensive expenditures. Costs of programs continue to increase radically, and political and managerial interest in cost per benefit has increased accordingly. Given this situation, the need for evaluation research has expanded.

The cost-benefit analyses and budgeting systems currently used at the federal level ideally should be developed on the basis of the outcome of experimental studies. What is typically done, however, is to estimate direct and indirect costs as well as direct and indirect savings, and then to examine the choices in these terms. The policy maker may not accept the ranking of alternatives prepared for him because he gives priority to political or other considerations; nevertheless, they serve as a yardstick. The problem in the estimation of efficiency in terms of cost-benefit *without* experimental data is that it must be based upon assumptions about efficacy. For example, suppose we know that if all automobile riders wore seat belts, deaths from auto accidents would be reduced by 20 per cent. Still, the hypothesis that a driver-education program would increase the number of persons wearing seat belts and thus reduce mortality is based upon the assumption that the driver-education type of program is efficacious.

Although many individuals use quite conservative estimates for arriving at their assumptions, their own biases and views regarding one program or another can affect the degree of conservatism they employ in such assumptions. This is of course less true in evaluation research. In a provocative paper on this point, Wildavsky (1967) tries to place into proper perspective the utilization of the concept of efficiency in decision making in the social-welfare, education, and health fields. He stresses that this concept is only one of the inputs which the policy maker must take into account in reaching a decision. He also argues strongly that there is some risk that efficiency will become the overriding criterion in the decision-making process. Nevertheless, as policy research progresses, much more attention will undoubtedly be paid to this concept and to those related in it, such as cost-per-benefit analysis (Freeman and Sherwood, 1965).

Other measures of efficiency, however, can be used as well: e.g., the number of hours of the practitioner's time; the future productivity, in financial or other terms, of the individuals involved as clients or patients; or the reduction in need for certain kinds of treatment or facilities. The particular instance should determine whether one is concerned with dollar costs, some unit of change, or hours of professional time. The important point is that measurement of efficiency is of critical importance, for it may be, as we saw earlier, that the program having the greatest dollar cost per unit was actually the most efficient in obtaining improvement.

In discussing the concept of efficacy, we have already referred to the need for denominators. Value judgments also play an important role in decisions about whether a program's efficacy is great enough to warrant its continuation. A reading program may demonstrate that children improve an average of one month in reading skill over a year's time period, as compared to a control group. A reading test may show that the group exposed to the program has an average reading score of 7.4 months in the eighth grade and 7.5 months in the ninth grade, in comparison to the control group, which remained at 7.4 months. Yet, if the norm for the test indicates a national average of 8.0, it becomes quite difficult to accept this program as an efficient one. In many cases, however, comparable norms are not available: the question then is whether to set some arbitrary criteria on the basis of values or to compare the program with others. In order to do the latter, we use dollar cost per unit of change.

A Comment on the Relationships Among Planning, Development and Implementation, and Evaluation

In introducing the discussion of the various aspects of social policy, we emphasized the overlap between various tasks and pointed out that the separation of the work on a program into planning, development, execution, and evaluation is to some extent artificial. Obviously, they are interdependent. Evaluation, as we have said, cannot take place when planning and program development have not been thoroughly undertaken. Unless both an impact model and the characteristics of a target population have been explicated, it is impossible to observe to what extent programs are conforming to the expectations of the program's developers. A knowledge of the target population and the impact model are absolutely necessary if one is going to design an evaluation experiment.

In developing an evaluation experiment, the researcher's task is to transform the program's plan into an experiment. The various statements that link together the program's elements into an impact model become the hypotheses that the policy researcher tests. The inputs or innovative procedures included in the program model represent the stimuli that he is seeking to evaluate. In the same sense, unless planning has been adequate, there is little basis on which to develop outcome measures or criteria. Thus, while the researcher may concentrate on one particular research task, he must recognize the interdependence of the various phases of policy development and research activity.

Chapter 6

THE COLLECTION OF DATA

In terms of craft or technique, the methodology of the social-policy researcher is fundamentally the same as that of other researchers in the social sciences. Surveys, analyses of recorded information, field and semi-participant observations, and experimental investigations all have their place. There are, however, some differences in the extent to which various methods are used, as well as some special limitations and difficulties in applying them. While no attempt will be made here to provide a thorough exposition of research methods, an effort to indicate some of the special considerations involved is in order, and to do so requires some general discussion of method.

Research methodology can be viewed as consisting of two highly interrelated but nevertheless distinct components: gathering data and analyzing data. A primary function of social-policy research is to obtain information and to draw inferences from it as an aid to the decision-making process. It should be apparent that the validity of the inferences is highly dependent upon the quality of the data utilized, but the interdependence is in fact even greater than it seems: ideally, the data-gathering procedures should be designed from the point of view of the kinds of inferences desired. This ideal is perhaps most fully realized in experimental studies. Nevertheless, data gathered by each of the techniques to be discussed below can be used, with varying degrees of validity and success, to make each of the basic types of inference—descriptive, predictive, and causal.

Each of the data-gathering procedures will be given brief introductory treatment; then, the analysis of data obtained by these methods will be discussed. However, since measurement is fundamental to both data gathering and data analysis, some of the concepts and problems involved in measurement will be presented first.

Measurement

A fundamental principle underlying all data gathering is classification. Phenomena are grouped or distinguished according to some conceptualized characteristic, and classifications are then set up in terms of the exhaustive set of categories of which the characteristic consists. Generally, these categories may be conceived of as ordered or unordered. An example of a characteristic for which the categories are usually viewed as unordered is sex, the *unordered categories* being male and female. *Ordered categories* are in positional relationship to each other, the positions based on the notion of "greater than" and "less than," as in an age distribution. Three types of ordered categories are differentiated, depending on whether the distances between the positions or categories are regarded as equal and whether the dimension has a true zero point.

Rankings and Ratings

Ranking systems, which are one type of ordered sets of categories or positions, assume neither equal intervals between positions nor a true zero point. *Ratings* may or may not have equal intervals or true zero points. In almost all cases, however, investigators strive for the most powerful type of measure, which has both equal intervals among the positions and a true zero. The ordinary 12-inch ruler and the bathroom scale meet these criteria.

Measurement in this broadest sense consists of classifying individuals, objects, events, and conditions, into one or another of the positions or categories of a particular characteristic. At one extreme, there may be only two unordered categories, as in sex. Race and religion represent similar, but somewhat more complicated, characteristics with corresponding sets of categories. At the other extreme, there may be an infinite set of ordered positions, as in length and weight. But basically the process is the same: measurement procedures permit the investigator to place each case into a category.

COUNTING

Another fundamental principle of all data gathering is counting. Once the phenomena have been classified, a count is taken of the number of cases falling in each category. All the statistical operations that enable us to draw inferences are based on the count (the number of cases) in each category and on the quantitative or measurement relationships, if any, among the categories.

SAMPLING

A major consideration in all data gathering is the sampling procedure. In any enquiry, there is an explicit or implicit population or phenomenon toward which the enquiry is directed, but only rarely can all the members of the population be studied. A sample of one sort or another is therefore involved. How that sample is drawn vitally affects the kinds of inferences that the data will permit. Differences among various polls of political opinion and between opinion polls and elections are largely due to the sampling. However, since sampling is more related to inference making than to data gathering itself, a more detailed discussion will be reserved for our subsequent treatment of data analysis and inference. It is mentioned here because the problem of sampling must be met before the data can be gathered.

VALIDITY

A key problem in measurement is whether valid information about the individual or situation has been obtained. *Validity* refers to the congruence between measures and the concepts that underlie them; in simple terms, does the instrument measure what it is supposed to measure? In part, the validity of a measure depends upon the means and procedures used to obtain information about the variable. Special problems are involved when data is being gathered by one human being (the data collector) from another human being (the subject or informant), as in surveys, clinical case studies, participant observation studies, field studies, and often even in experiments. An important issue in such situations is whether or not the "right" question has been asked, the one which in fact enables us to measure a characteristic or phenomenon. The setting, as well as the character of the relationship between the informant and the data collector, are also likely to influence the validity of the information obtained.

RELIABILITY

Reliability, in its simplest form, refers to the prospects for obtaining consistent and similar measurements when the data collection procedure is replicated. It should be pointed out that, regardless of other aspects of the research endeavor, if a study is unreliable, it is worthless. Sophistication and theoretical elegance in other phases are of no value if the data are unreliable. In its broadest form, reliability may be thought of in terms of correlations between rankings. If the same characteristic is measured two or more times, the reliability of the measuring procedures can be judged by estimating the extent of the relative positions of each case from one measurement to another. Reliability, in a narrower sense, refers to the extent to which the cases remain, from measurement to measurement, in the same positional category in the set of categories for that characteristic. Reliability in the first sense makes no assumptions about true measures or values for the phenomena measured, but only about relative positions.

It may help to think of measures as estimates, and of measurement as the process which produces estimates. In this sense, measurement is undertaken either to estimate the relative position of a phenomenon within a population of phenomena on some particular characteristic, or to estimate the particular category into which that phenomenon falls with respect to some particular characteristic. Ranking people as to income is an illustration of the first; classifying persons as white or black, of the second. In either case, conceived in this way, reliability is a quality of the estimate rather than of the measuring procedures. This can be seen rather easily, since it is generally agreed that reliability usually increases as one increases the number of observations or the size of the group studied. It should be obvious that since repeated or wider use of an instrument cannot improve its reliability, it must be *the reliability of the estimate* which is improved by the repeated or wider use of a particular set of measuring procedures.

The notion of reliability as the reliability of estimates of relative positions within a set of ordered categories is generally only applicable to ordered variables without equal intervals or true zero points. Aptitude for a particular task or occupation is an example of such a variable. A highly reliable estimate in this sense would be one which is based on a set of measuring procedures which have been demonstrated, upon repeated use, to rank the members of a population the same or very nearly the same with respect to a particular characteristic. Aptitude scores might change, but their relative positions would remain the same.

For unordered variables, and ordered variables with equal intervals between categories, we use a narrower and somewhat more useful concept of reliability. A highly reliable estimate, in this sense, is one in which the prospects are high that the same individual, upon repeated measurement, will be placed in the same or very nearly the same category with respect to a particular characteristic. This is rather easily seen in the case of unordered variables such as sex and religion. When the variables are more complex, it may be helpful to introduce the notion of precision.

Generally, there will be variability among the estimates produced by repeated efforts to measure the same phenomena. *Precision* refers to the variability among estimates: the less the variability, the more precise the estimate; and the more precise the estimate, the more reliable it will be, in this second, narrower concept of reliability. It is also generally true that more precise estimates will be more reliable in the first, broader sense of reliability, in that they will provide reliable measurements of relative positions among specific populations.

BIAS AND ACCURACY

It should be noted at this point that reliability and precision are essentially independent of the important notions of validity and accuracy. *Accuracy* is the inverse of bias. Accuracy assumes, theoretically at least, that there is a true value of the phenomenon being measured. *Bias* is the extent to which the average value of a series of measurements tends to approach a value other than the true value as the number of estimates increases. It is quite possible to have a highly reliable, highly precise, and even valid estimate which is inaccurate. To take a relatively simple example, if one attempts to determine the average height of a particular population and each individual is measured from the floor while standing on a two-inch board, there would be definite bias in the estimate. The average value of the measurements would not approach the true value, but a value two inches greater. Despite the bias, if reasonable care were taken in the rest of the measuring operations, reliable and precise estimates would result. They would also be valid estimates in at least two senses of the terms (1) it is definitely height which is being measured, and not something else—weight, neuroticism or so on; and (2) to the extent that height is known to correlate with or predict some other phenomena, the estimates should predict them as well as true ones. But they would be definitely inaccurate estimates.

In the simple example used, the bias is easily discoverable and, in addition, measurable. In most social-science enquiries, unfortunately, bias is much less easily discovered and is generally not measurable in the same sense. Bias is, for example, a serious problem in the wording of questionnaires and interview schedules. It is an even more difficult problem to handle in the conduct of actual interviews.

It also should be apparent that it is possible to have reliable, precise, and even accurate estimates which are not necessarily valid. If, for example, the quantity of perspiration in the palm of the hand is used as a measure of anxiety, reliable, precise, and accurate estimates of the quantity of perspiration may be produced. Those estimates may have nothing to do with anxiety, however. That is a question of validity, which must be demonstrated independently of the quality of the estimates of the quantity of perspiration in the palm.

In social-policy research, each of these matters—reliability, precision, accuracy, bias, and of course validity—are very important, because work undertaken on relatively small study groups may and often are extrapolated to entire communities. There is a vast and growing body of literature dealing with the recognition and handling of these problems with which the policy researcher should become at least familiar. Elinson (1963) for example, has specified a number of different types and sources of unreliability. In surveys, the problems include ambiguity of the item or question, difficulties in communication occasioned by noise or obstructions, and even the ineptness of the interviewer in reading the question.

The availability of standard tests and measuring instruments varies from field to field. Psychologists have developed many more standard tests to measure variables of interest to them than have sociologists. There are a number of batteries, for example, to measure personality characteristics and to assess performance in reading, motor, and other skills. Standard scales to measure sociological characteristics are much more difficult to find, although several compendiums of frequently used instruments are now available (Miller, 1964). It is the responsibility of the policy researcher to maintain his familiarity with developments in methodology and measuring instruments.

Data Gathering

THE SURVEY

The survey is the primary means by which empirical data on social life and social relations have been gathered (Hyman, 1955). In its most traditional and common form, the survey is used as a means of systematically describing an individual's views, opinions, attitudes and, sometimes, behavior. In the form of public-opinion polls, surveys have received popular recognition because of their use at election time and because commercial organizations employ them in making marketing de-

cisions. Politicians, from the President of the United States to city coun-
cilmen, have found continuing audits and analyses of the views of citizens
or selected groups in the community to be useful in the development of
programs. It has also been possible, through surveys, to obtain considerable data about a broad range of behavior.

The Uses of Surveys in Policy Research. Surveys continue to be
quite common, but recently their use in social-policy research has expanded. The types of behavior examined have covered a broad range:
for example, much of our estimates of the sexual conduct of Americans
is derived from studies known by the name of the principal investigator,
Kinsey (Kinsey, Pomeroy, and Martin, 1948). Estimates of the "true" incidence of crime have been sought by interviewing representative samples
of community residents and asking them to report occasions when they
have been victimized, i.e., experienced crime themselves. There are studies
in which high-school students have given self-reports of their delinquent
behavior (Nye and Short, 1957). Increasingly, surveys are being used to
obtain estimates of behavior, as well as to seek out opinions, views, and
attitudes. Both these types of descriptive information have served in examinations of the extent of deviation from prescribed roles or norms.

Survey research studies have provided the data for many of the correlational analyses crucial to the planning process. In some cases, they
supply the independent or predictor variable which is then correlated
with the information about the dependent variable obtained from other
sources. For example, census information about the social characteristics of residents of different census tracts has been correlated with rates of
deviance such as delinquency and suicide. This information is employed to test various hypotheses about the etiology of deviance and to
determine the residential perimeters of target populations.

Finally, surveys have been used in certain natural situations, quasi-
experiments, to examine the impact of events on populations. For example, following riots in several cities, Spiegel and his associates (Lemberg
Center for the Study of Violence, 1967) interviewed representative samples
of whites and Negroes in three riot-torn cities and in three cities selected
as controls because they approximated the riot-torn communities except
for the absence of widespread violence. The attempt was to identify the
causal characteristics of the violence.

Types of Surveys. Typically, highly structured instruments are used
in surveys, with a prescribed ordering of items and a series of standardized
questions to which the informant responds. However, there are other
ways of eliciting information. These range from projective techniques
similar to the thematic aptitude tests psychologists use with individuals
to "depth," rather than structured, interviews (Richardson, Dohrenwend
and Klein, 1965).

One argument in defense of depth interviews is that direct questioning will not penetrate below the superficial, public responses of individuals. When it is thought that concealment of real feelings and views will result, a more subtle and indirect approach is used. For example, some investigators question whether interviewers are reasonably responsive to questions about marital happiness and family relations in a structured interview. Another argument for unstructured survey instruments is that the investigator may start out with less than a full view of his problem. Free responses may lead to an expansion of his perspective and to further development, refinement, and amplification of his area of inquiry. Such interviews are a stimulus to the investigator and his team as well as a means of eliciting information. Suppose one is concerned, for instance, with the range of reactions of individuals to drugs such as LSD. It is argued that no body of literature exists which codifies the range of responses to the drugs and that it is incumbent upon the investigator to probe deeply in order to obtain an adequate description of the range.

Concern about the validity of responses to structured items is perhaps greatest when the objective of the study is to obtain information about the personal conduct of the informants. While the point has merit, it is easy to become overly skeptical. Well-constructed studies in which there have been separate and external validating sources of information about such sensitive subjects as sexual behavior, emotional illness, or reports of embarrassing situations tend to show an encouraging consistency between responses and data collected by other means.

In part, the degree of structure of a survey should depend upon the intended use of the data, in part, it depends upon opportunity. Zelditch (1962), in his discussion of various approaches to data collection, has attempted to develop a framework for selecting the method best suited to the purpose (Table 6.1), and also points out the special uses of the survey.

Surveying Problem Groups. Thus far, we have indicated types of problems which plague all research. These difficulties may intervene a bit more sharply in social-policy research because of the purposes of the work and the limitations on time and on developmental and design efforts. Much of social-policy research is carried on because of the particular problems, within a community, of the poor, the troubled, and the socially or physically incompetent. Studies of a total community compound all of the problems we have mentioned, especially when unusual and unique groups constitute the target population.

Rapport. Particularly in the structured interview in survey studies, it is important that there be rapport between the informant and the interviewer. *Rapport* refers to the development of an interpersonal relationship between the informant and interviewer so that the elicitor of the data has confidence in the information recalled. It is generally held that

TABLE 6.1

Methods of Obtaining Information

	Enumerations and Samples	Participant Observation	Interviewing Informants
Frequency distributions	Prototype and best form	Usually inadequate and ineffective	Often, but not always, inadequate; if adequate, it is efficient
Incidents, histories	Not adequate by itself; not efficient	Prototype and best form	Adequate, with precautions, and efficient
Institutionalized norms and statuses	Adequate but inefficient	Adequate, but inefficient except for unverbalized norms	Most efficient and hence best form

FROM: Morris Zelditch, Jr., "Some Methodological Problems of Field Studies," *American Journal of Sociology*, March 1962. Reprinted with permission from the University of Chicago Press.

the interview situation is a good one when the informant and the interviewer feel comfortable with each other and have a common language and frame of reference.

Studies of information collection reveal that the informant-interviewer relationship and the social and personal characteristics of both parties interact and affect the quality and quantity of material elicited, the willingness of informants to be interviewed, and the length of interviews. An analysis of the staff of the National Opinion Research Center, one of the most highly regarded academically oriented interviewing groups, shows that interviewers are usually unrepresentative of the target population. Their national interviewing staff tends to be female, middle-class, and disproportionately Jewish. Whether such individuals relate well to the Puerto Rican, the Negro, or the poor is a troublesome question (Dohrenwend, Colombatos, and Dohrenwend, 1968).

The Character of Survey Instruments. Another communication problem in surveys of special groups arises from the ways that instruments have been developed. Most of our standardized instruments and measures reflect the middle-class orientation of the investigators; moreover, they are often pre-tested on persons who have a fairly large vocabulary.

Many of the commonly used terms may be difficult, if not entirely impossible, for the informants to understand.

Survey instruments designed to elicit information about values and attitudes, contain items that would be taken seriously by middle-class informants but that may seem ludicrous and unrealistic to lower-class informants. Some of the questions on child rearing, food habits, and work relationships which are repeatedly used in studies of middle-income families may have no or little meaning for problem groups. Couch and Keniston (1960) discovered that all informants, but more particularly lower-income and less-educated ones, experience boredom, fatigue, or lack of understanding during the interview—a result of some combination of poor rapport and inappropriate instrumentation. These feelings may account for what is technically termed "response set" or the development of a yea-saying pattern: the informant, rather than pleading "I don't know" or terminating the interview, takes the course of responding "yes" to virtually every item he answers. Studies tend to show that low-income and uneducated individuals are much more likely to overconform and to be overconcerned with the reactions of the interviewers to their behavior and views. Conforming responses, or at least responses that the informants believe will conform to the norms and values of the interviewers, tend to replace responses based on the attitudes and opinions really held by the informants (Edward, 1957).

Innovations in Data Collection. Social-policy researchers are often blasé about conditions affecting interviews. They presume, with impunity, that these factors do not make a difference in the information they obtain. At present, we do not know enough to solve some of the problems—how to modify interviewing styles, or how to train and make use of interviewers with backgrounds similar to those of the informants. Furthermore, studies suggest that identification between informant and interviewer, e.g. as between a Negro interviewer and interviewee, can introduce biases as well. The solution, according to some researchers, is not simply to "match" the interviewer to the informant, but to reduce the social distance between the two to a "moderate extent." In other words, it is equally undesirable to have an over-identified interviewer as it is to have an unidentified one. A useful procedure is to use different "types" of interviewers during a pilot or pre-test phase, with a random assignment of informants to them, and then to estimate differences in response. Another, more economical but less definitive means of examining the effect of the interviewer is to study refusal rates, that is, to return to a pilot sample of informants and gauge their reactions to the interviewer and the interview situation and to solicit the reaction of the interviewers themselves.

Most important perhaps, we often do not know how to frame questions, probes, and guides in ways that will be meaningful to particular cultural and ethnic groups and to people of different classes and educational levels. Measures of alienation, anomie, emotional status, and occupational aspiration may all require revision or modification for use in studies of special groups. As with the problem of improving reliability, and indeed what is being discussed is one source of unreliability, much more methodological work must be done. In recent years, some of the programs requiring survey research directed at special problem groups have employed indigenous community members as data collectors (Weiss, 1968). In part, this has been a product of community organization efforts, and in part it is due to a belief that improved data collection will result. The use of community members as data collectors has been reported successful to some extent, but there are risks involved as well. Informants may be reluctant to communicate certain information to people from the same community. They may feel that the interviewer is likely to use their information as gossip. Also, within certain neighborhoods there may be marked schisms in social relationships, schisms which could be more detrimental to the data-collection process than discrepancies in class and status between investigators and study-group members. In one study conducted in a predominantly black community, for example, the investigators were unaware that there was sharp antagonism between persons who had migrated to the United States from the West Indies and those who were old residents of the community. Such a difficulty requires sensitivity and astuteness on the part of the social-policy investigator and, it is worth emphasizing, is reason for him to support methodological inquiries.

Not only are surveys important, but continuing audits are also useful. Studies requiring repeated interviews over a period of time enable us to examine changing attitudes, behavior, and conditions in the community. Over the years we have developed sophistication in the design of studies, beginning with a now classic investigation on voting behavior in which a panel of community members was interviewed before and after an election (Lazarsfeld et al., 1948). In some cases, it is necessary to return to the same individuals; in others, it is only necessary to obtain equivalent study groups and to reinterview different but matched groups at various times.

The latter approach, although it renders impossible comparisons of change in individuals, has the advantage of minimizing the accumulation of refusals. It is a general rule of thumb that competent surveys can obtain information on between 90 and 95 per cent of the study group (Freeman and Simmons, 1960). Even if this is so, however, the additive effect of returning to the same informants, say three or four times, may result in a loss rate of some 15 to 30 per cent of the original study group. For this reason, the use of parallel samples often is thought to be desirable.

Loss of Informants. In studies of individuals afflicted with many social problems, the difficulties encountered are intense compared with studies of the general population. In repeat-interview investigations, the high rate of residential mobility in low-income areas presents acute problems. Mobility has to be taken into account in specifying the size of the original sample and in the design of the investigation; otherwise, losses from the study group may make the investigation useless.

Another problem is that some aspects of social disorganization require the most carefully developed definitions in order to sample adequately and to carry out the study. In low-income areas, for example, names often do not appear in either a building directory or on mailboxes, hence it is hard to draw samples and to locate informants by name. Frequently, interviewers in the field have to be innovative. Then, too, in areas in which there is a pooling of living arrangements, where several families are in one household, the problem of what constitutes the family unit must be dealt with. It is not unusual, for instance, for two families receiving aid for families with dependent children to reside in the same household.

Problems in the development of survey methods for problem groups have their analogs in the study of other groups. There is increasing interest, as part of social-policy investigations, in identifying and examining the views and behavior of various specialized groups, including groups which have power in the community. A considerable controversy exists over the means of identifying community leaders, for example (Walton, 1966). Some argue that the general reputation of individuals constitutes a useful means of identifying leaders; others would use measures of behavior, such as membership on boards or community groups, to rate influence. A third approach is to employ some index of either prestige or socioeconomic status. The social-policy researcher must exercise considerable care in deciding how to select persons for a study of community power.

Finally, like the special problems of interviewing low-income people or people living in areas of disorganization, there are difficulties in interviewing members of the elite, important businessmen, political figures, and the like (Smigel, 1964). One solution is to interview them when they are least occupied with work or during the lunch hour. Again, the characteristics of the interviewer are important.

Studies of Records

A virtually inexhaustible supply of information exists in the records of the many agencies and organizations in the various sectors of the health, education, and welfare field. Various action-demonstration programs and continuing research operations also have developed record-keeping procedures (Cline, Freeman, and Wheeler, 1968). As an illustration, in order to obtain descriptive data about the incidents and circumstances surrounding child abuse, a research project sponsored by the Children's Bureau has developed a uniform record form now employed in a large number of states (Gil, 1968).

It is important to distinguish between records designed primarily for the convenience and use of practitioners and records that, while they may have this function as well, have been designed as research instruments (Robins, 1966). An illustration of the latter is provided in a report of a project which developed a computerized program for processing the reports of detached workers. The project concerned delinquency prevention among young men and women in several high-delinquency areas of a large city (Cline, Freeman, and Wheeler, 1968). The collaborative procedure provided a ready means for the agency to examine the work of individual workers and permitted the presentation of consolidated reports about the agency's efforts to the sponsoring public body. At the same time, information could be presented to the school system and to agencies of social control. Finally, the accumulation of data in systematic fashion, along with ready access to the data provided by storage on a computer tape, made feasible a wide variety of investigations of a more academic but nevertheless social-policy character.

Undoubtedly, if the policy researcher is going to persuade social agencies to develop their own record-keeping systems so as to maximize their research value, he must demonstrate that the necessary procedures do not distract from the operation of the agency. He must also prove that these procedures will not create any great increase in amount of work.

The availability of computers and punch-card equipment should encourage the development of new record-keeping systems rather than the continuance of narrative files. In some places, researchers are encouraging consortiums of operating agencies to pool their resources and maintain a single, over-all computerized record-keeping system. Such consortium-sponsored uniform record-keeping procedures could easily be converted to a data bank mentioned earlier in this volume for a particular community or about a particular area of concern.

THE LIMITATIONS OF RECORDS

Many social-research investigators are aware of the limited quality of information available on records and are critical of their use for research purposes, particularly records maintained by practitioners. One criticism of information collected by agencies is that the procedures and types of items collected are often based on custom and ritual. Information which hasn't made sense to anyone in a half-century may still be included on a particular record form. Along the same line, many agencies that have a psychiatric orientation and individualized treatment programs require narrative summaries of cases. Frequently, there is no auditing or quality-control of these materials; they are practically useless for research purposes. In certain settings, the continual storage of information without any systematic attempts to review the files results in an overload of paper, making it impossible to filter through to the meaningful portions of the records for research purposes.

Large agencies and institutions engaged in preventive and treatment programs have, by and large, failed to take advantage of computer and punch card systems. Data remains in many instances practically inaccessible. However, where a well-developed computer system has been put into effect, the data has proven to be of considerable value to people engaged in social-policy research. For example, a significant amount of utilization data on health care, particularly on the hospital experience of persons, has been collected because of the quite sophisticated data collection, storage, and analysis system of the Blue Cross and Blue Shield groups (American Hospital Association, 1962 and on).

Another limitation on the use of records is the lack of rationality in collection procedures and in the items selected. In many cases, the problem can be solved if the particular agency would ask itself what it needs to know, and why. In other cases, the proper information is obtained, but the problem of recording it is not examined from the standpoint of the network of interlocking groups who either are or may be involved in the future with particular clients or patients.

An equally severe problem is that record-keeping procedures must be monitored and that people have to be trained for this responsibility. Surveillance procedures are essential, to ensure the usefulness of the records in social research in general and their utility in terms of the practical goals of the agency. Unfortunately, surveillance of record-keeping procedures is rare. Practitioners are often apathetic about records; their attitude is that record keeping interferes with their work.

UNIFORM REPORTING

The recognition of the importance of records has led to attempts in the health, education, and welfare fields to develop uniform-reporting schemes. The development of social indicators, referred to in an earlier chapter, requires such uniform procedures. Many of these schemes are voluntary, and there is doubt about their adequate functioning in the long term. Nevertheless, as an illustration, one may take the reporting program in the field of mental health developed by the National Institutes of Mental Health (Bahn, 1961). A number of states have agreed to a uniform means of counting patients under treatment for mental disorders, with considerable consequent improvement in our knowledge of the prevalence of mental illness and the characteristics of those afflicted.

Another illustration of the benefits of uniform reporting is the effort of the Department of Justice to develop uniform crime reports. The cooperation of many police departments has been important to the success of the endeavor, although there still are major problems about the uniformity of police returns (Skolnick, 1966). Both the proportion of crimes that come to police attention and the differences in the administration of justice limit the utility of crime statistics.

There is much criticism of the precision and reliability of both local and national estimates. It is fair to say that we know too little about the volume of crime in the United States, despite the funds expended for crime control and our concern with the problem (President's Commission on Law Enforcement and Administration of Justice, 1967). At state and local levels, information is conspicuously absent on deviant behavior, physical and mental illness, the characteristics of social control, and treatment settings. A tremendous waste results from our lack of information, and special studies are necessary.

At the present time, there are also problems of conceptualization which limit and hinder the collection and compilation of data. Many terms commonly used in the practicing professions defy operational definition; consequently there is a great deal of variability from place to place and from time to time in the meaning of measures. The need for valid operational definitions plagues the health field. The most commonplace terms, e.g., "bedside nursing-care" and "medical supervision," have no consistent meaning for the many individuals who have to report figures on them.

Case Studies

The analysis of an individual case and the comparison of a number of cases are important methodological approaches to understanding social behavior and social processes. Although case studies may not always provide the kind of evidence needed for decision making, they prove exceedingly valuable to social-policy research at several points. Case studies provide the insights required to bring the problem into focus and develop the framework for a study. They are also highly useful in illustrating and supplementing statistical reports. Particularly when the analytical skills of policy makers is limited, illustrative narratives can emphasize the meaningfulness of findings and inferences. Finally, studies of deviant cases provide additional insights and serve as stimuli for the development of additional studies. They also suggest the further specification and tailoring of action programs to coincide with the needs of subgroups or individuals.

The danger of good case-study materials is that their overwhelmingly dramatic quality can obscure their limited general applicability. Moreover, by their very nature they can be highly subjective, representing more a tool of persuasion than an objective research analysis.

In many areas of concern, the investigator has insufficient knowledge about the conditions, processes, and behavior he intends to study. If, for example, a researcher wants to investigate the Hippie movement, he should spend some time gathering case material. He should gain an insight into and some understanding of the attitudes, beliefs and practices that characterize the Hippie. Illustrations and case studies would be an exceedingly valuable addition to a statistical report on conditions in neighborhoods where the Hippies live, or on their behavior.

We have said that many leads have been derived from case studies. A classic example of the use of case studies at the start of a broad investigation is the well-known investigation of the authoritarian personality by Adorno and his associates (1950). Commissioned shortly after World War II by a leading Jewish social-action organization, the study was planned to provide some understanding of the problems of prejudice. Of particular interest was the relationship between personality and prejudice, and a sizable number of case studies were made in order to identify items to be included in personality scales developed for a large sample survey, the most famous being the "F" scale measure of authoritarianism.

PROBLEMS IN CASE STUDIES

A considerable amount of effort has gone into developing methods of systematically undertaking comparative analyses of cases, as well as into providing procedures for making longitudinal case studies. In certain fields, such as mental health, several teams of investigators have used a longitudinal approach to examine and review the posthospital care of the mental patient and to suggest programmatic improvements (Simmons, 1967). Such longitudinal studies generally are based on the assumption that, with time as a variable, the changes in the social processes of the patient can provide an understanding of his posthospital experience.

In a sense, most case studies are longitudinal, although the information usually is gathered on an *ex post facto* basis. As one moves back into the life of the individual or the environment that is the subject of the analysis, however, the specificity and quality of the data diminishes. Prospective longitudinal studies, often advanced as the most desirable means of gathering information about processes, suffer many of the same kinds of problems as panel survey studies, including loss of cases.

Both longitudinal and comparative case studies rest on the assumption that it is possible to compare similar material of particular concern to the researcher. In longitudinal case studies, the emphasis is usually on comparing the data at one point in time with the data at another point in time; in comparative studies, one individual's behavior or situation is compared with another's. Several problems limit the extent to which such efforts have been satisfactorily carried out. One is that nondirected interviews are commonly used. Even when the interviews are relatively focused and data guides are employed, the level and depth of the information may vary from case to case, and indeed typically does. Consequently, the investigator may be comparing a relatively superficial and bland response with a detailed and perhaps affect-laden response. The development of systematic interviewing procedures through training the interviewer and more closely specifying the required data is important work still to be done (Geer, 1964).

Field Investigations

An alternative to asking people what they do—the approach of surveys and case studies—is to observe what they do; such observation is generally called a *field study*. Field investigators employ the interview as well. Rarely does the observer have enough acumen and sophistication to be able to interpret all of what he sees without questioning the participants; he also often wishes to place what he sees within the context of the events preceding the period of observation. Field studies are traditional in social research, and many of the early investigations of an empirical sort in American sociology were of a field-study type. In social-policy research, a variety of recent field investigations has proved most stimulating and innovative.

Field workers vary in their approach, and styles of field studies differ markedly. At one extreme, the investigator becomes a participant in the activities and relationships of group members (Caudill, 1958). At the other extreme, the field worker tags along but remains relatively detached from the activities of the group, retreating to a corner where he remains unobserved but observing. In studies of mental hospitals, individual researchers have actually assumed the patient's role or have tried to disappear into the woodwork (Stanton and Schwartz, 1954). Somewhere in between the two extremes lies the most common method, wherein the investigator is a "semi-participant observer." He picks and chooses his role in terms of his own personal skills, his self-evaluation, and the acceptance of the group. In certain circumstances, he participates; in others, he does not. In studies of medical education, for example, the investigator attended classes and even took examinations with the students, but he did not participate in certain of their clinical activities (Becker et al., 1966).

THE USES OF FIELD STUDIES

In social-policy research, field studies have two key uses. They are essential in evaluation research, in order to estimate the extent to which the outlines of a program are actually carried out in the day-to-day operations of various agencies. As we have pointed out, it is foolish to evaluate nonexistent programs or to assess programs on the basis of a written plan when in actuality they are working out quite differently (Freeman and Sherwood, 1965). It is simply not possible to undertake adequate evaluation research without field investigations.

Field studies have another contribution to make to social-policy investigations. They are important to an understanding of how the practitioner works, making it possible to judge how much he deviates from the formal outlines of his role and to identify hitherto uncharted and unidentified activities. A striking illustration is contained in a recent book by Skolnick (1966) on the workings of the police. Skolnick records many instances in which police act as judge and jury, making decisions about illegal and unlawful behavior as they control crime. Another illustration along the same lines is Wilson's comparative field study (1968) of several police forces. He attempts to demonstrate that policemen bring together their own backgrounds and education and the ideological orientation of their particular force.

We do not have enough information about how the various health, education, and welfare organizations, as well as the persons in them, actually operate. What policy makers think professionals and specialists do is often very different from what they actually do. Few policy makers, for instance, are intimately aware of what goes on in prisons, what life is like in a delinquency institution or hospital, or how union executives operate. Extensive and continual field investigations are required. This is an area of social-policy research that clearly is underdeveloped.

PROBLEMS IN METHOD

There are several reasons for the limited number of craftsmanlike field studies in social-policy research. To begin with, the general limitations of field investigations apply when they are undertaken for social-policy investigations. In many ways, the general problems are similar to those discussed in the section on case studies. Much of what the field worker does is not codified; thus, the difficulties of team research, in which several settings are viewed by different people, are severe. The problems of data analysis relevant to case studies pertain to field studies as well. Since the noteworthy work of Whyte, *Street Corner Society* (1955), a number of efforts have been made to specify the process of field work and some of the problems to which the field worker must be sensitive.

Attempts have been made to teach how to be a field worker in a systematic manner. Geer (1964), for example, tries to describe what the first days in the field are like. She discusses the process the field worker goes through in moving from general, often oversimplified hypotheses to more specific and useful ones. It is encouraging that observations made from many settings in field studies apparently do from time to time converge. In one study (Geer et al., 1968) of "learning the ropes," a group of field workers independently concluded that the peer group of students, regardless of whether they are interns in a high-status medical hospital or students in a barber college, contributes greatly to the learning experience during the early days in the setting.

It is possible, in evaluation research, to circumvent some of the limitations of the field method by developing observational forms of a quantitative character. For example, one might be able to indicate the actual deviations, both qualitatively and quantitatively, from the program as specified. Fairly sophisticated sampling methods are also feasible. Some of the concepts of time-and-motion studies (Miller and Bryant, 1964) can provide rigor and economy in the field.

For a long time, there has been a conflict in social-science research between those who do surveys, the quantitatively oriented researchers, and the qualitatively oriented field workers. In academic sociology, the schism persists, to some degree, but in social-policy research there is little possibility of taking an extreme position. On one hand, surveys and evaluation studies must, of necessity, be concerned with quantitative measurement. On the other hand, field investigations are essential, both for understanding the work of the practitioner and for the checking up that is part of evaluation research. No one, unfortunately, has yet been able to provide the same rigorous level of training for field workers as can be given to individuals engaged in other modes of data collection.

One limitation of field work is the general view, not necessarily borne out by research data, that field workers must be highly educated, theoretically sophisticated, and strongly identified with an academic discipline. While it is historically true that most field work has been lone-wolf scholarship, there is reason to question the merit of this stance. If each evaluation and each descriptive study of the work of practitioners must be undertaken by a full-fledged, completely trained sociologist or anthropologist, then the opportunities for pursuing such work are severely curtailed. Given the demand for field workers, it is necessary to make use of research assistants as data collectors. In several current investigations, efforts are being made to provide training and insight into the particular problems of field work to individuals with at least an undergraduate degree in one of the social sciences (Warren, 1969). If it proves possible to gain additional field workers in this way, more evaluations can be undertaken and more will be learned about the various processes of interaction in the health, education, and welfare fields.

Experimental Research

Earlier, we pointed out that opportunities to conduct experiments that are consistent with the canons of social research are extremely rare. A growing exception to this statement is the application of experimental designs in the evaluation of programs and practices in health, education, and welfare.

Evaluation research is probably the greatest challenge to the ingenuity of the social-policy researcher. If it is going to be well-designed, and be completed, we will have to solve the problems of establishing community relationships and maintaining the cooperation of the parties involved. In the previous discussion, we noted the need for impact models, i.e., the specification of input variables, of the impact sequence, and of the expected result. These models, whether extremely simple or quite complex, are implicit in the plans of the policy makers. One of the tasks of research is to participate in their explication.

EXPERIMENTAL DESIGN

In general, evaluation research is subject to the same rules as experiments undertaken in other fields (Edwards, 1962). Yet, certain special conditions plague the researcher in this area, among them difficult problems of control and randomization. Suchman (1967) is among those who argue that there are essentially two types of evaluation. He defines the extent to which programs meet the expectations of practitioners and other experts as being a form of evaluation. In a sense he is correct. However, this view of evaluation research circumvents the identification of the cause-and-effect relationship, which is critical in the development of adequate programming.

USE OF CONTROL GROUPS

In most life-science and agricultural studies from which many of the notions of experimental design are derived, the control group is typically referred to as the part of the study population which was left unexposed. The control group, thus, includes those who were not treated or those who were allowed to behave as they usually would.

In experimental research into social phenomena, it is necessary to explore what "unexposed" means. In a laboratory study using animals, the environment of the control group is equivalent to that of the study group. All conditions are duplicated, except that the control group is not exposed to the particular intervention which represents the independent variable or variables of the experiment. In certain types of human experimentation, a similar approach is used: for example, the patients may be in exactly the same environment, but some may receive a placebo while others receive a new drug.

In social-policy research conducted in the community, such a level of control over the unexposed group does not exist. The results must therefore be scrutinized closely in order to avoid misleading or mistaken inferences. In one evaluation study of a special weekend camp for children of low-income families, a random sample of a total number of applicants was sent to the camp. The applicants not sent to the camp were regarded as the control group. One measure of the outcome of the study was involvement with the law, measured by police contacts, and there was some indication that the adolescents in the camp had fewer contacts with the police than those who did not. An important question raised by these findings is whether it was the camp program, with its emphasis upon group participation and citizenship training, that accounted for the lower rate, or whether it was simply that the boys in the experimental group were in a supervised setting during the hours when the boys in the control group were on the streets. In such a case, the control group should either be similarly restricted in the hours they can come into contact with the police, or the rate of delinquency should be calculated in terms of hours of exposure to the ordinary environment. Then the efficacy of the program could be determined better. One difficulty in evaluation research and in the extension of findings to broad-scale programs is the inability, in many instances, to separate out the elements of the program which constitute the causal variables—as in the example just cited.

Another illustration of the problem of exposure can be found in an evaluation of a small residential program for the rehabilitation of delinquents. The key element supposedly was the group psychotherapy— referred to as "guided group interaction"—to which the boys were exposed (Freeman and Weeks, 1956). The control group consisted of boys institutionalized in a typical state training school. However, in addition to the guided group interaction, other differences existed. For example, the boys had to drive past an outmoded and vicious-looking training school in order to be transported to Highfields, the small residential experimental setting. Was it the relative size of the institution, the therapy, or some other extraneous environmental differences which was the causal element in the outcome? If this program is to be used in other settings, this question must be acknowledged at the policy level.

In large-scale programs, it is often not feasible to replicate the precise experimental circumstances which guided the original demonstration. Consequently, there is some risk involved in extrapolating from small experiments to broad-scale programs. One responsibility of the social-policy researcher is to warn of such uncontrolled differences. Another is that he must strongly promote the replication of evaluation studies as programs are carried out on the larger scale. Without any really good evaluation studies, for example, mental hospitals have been influenced and changed greatly by psychodynamic views. A recent study of the impact of a psychotherapeutic orientation on hospitalized mental patients, however, suggests that any positive result is probably a consequence of the smaller institutional size of psychotherapeutically oriented settings, rather than of the therapy itself (Ullmann, 1967).

BARRIERS TO EXPERIMENTS

Major barriers to more extensive evaluations are the uncontrolled loss of cases, the difficulty of randomization, and the problem of persuading practitioners and policy makers that it is desirable to withhold or provide substitute treatment for some part of a group.

Loss of Sample Cases. In most evaluation studies of community programs, the loss of sample cases is crucial. For example, an effort was made to evaluate the impact of providing good public housing (Wilner, 1962). From the total pool of eligible applicants, a random but representative selection was made. The rejected applicants constituted the control group. A significant number in the control group, however, did not remain in the inadequate housing in which they had lived at the outset of the investigation. On their own, they moved to more desirable quarters. In the analysis of the investigation, therefore, the loss of sample cases became an issue. Should the researchers have included the group who independently sought and obtained housing which might be equivalent to the housing provided the experimental group? To have left them out, of course, would have destroyed the comparability of the two groups; but to have kept them would have raised the question of whether or not the experiment is sensitive to the changes. Similarly, in evaluation studies conducted in school systems, individuals are lost to the study because their families move to another community or neighborhood and they do not remain part of the school's population.

Randomization. Randomization is difficult in most cases. Sometimes it is not practical, because practitioners and policy makers are reluctant to give up what they believe are their rightful responsibilities in making assignments. In the study of Highfields (Freeman and Weeks, 1956), the therapeutically oriented delinquency institution mentioned earlier, juvenile-court judges refused to allow the random assignment of boys, arguing that it was their prerogative to render decisions about who should be treated at Highfields, who should be placed on probation, and who should be institutionalized in a typical training school. Nevertheless, it was possible to randomize subjects in a similar effort to evaluate an institution for delinquents in Utah (Empey and Rabow, 1961).

There are, in randomization, other limitations necessitated by practical administrative difficulties. We have mentioned the investigation of the efficacy of teaching machines in the classroom. The workings of the school systems, frequently permit only the random assignment of classes, not individuals, to experimental and control groups. In such cases, the question is whether you have a sample based on the number of students or on the number of classes.

Another problem that harasses the evaluation researcher is the resistance of individuals who believe that evaluation denies treatment, or optimum treatment, to a portion of the population. Sometimes these critics try to terminate evaluation studies on the grounds that the impressionistic evidence of efficacy is sufficient. There is a fascinating sociological analysis, by Fox (1959), describing the pressures on a research team testing the efficacy of a new treatment for a disease: it was felt that they should terminate their experiment because of what apparently were the obvious benefits the experimental group was receiving from the new therapy. This problem will continue to plague investigators undertaking evaluation research. It is one of the major reasons why they must become sensitive to the problems of practice and ideology in particular fields.

Evaluation researchers have devised two strategies for handling negative reactions to control groups. One is to develop designs which do *not* rely on the test of treatment in comparison with no treatment, designs which compare an innovative treatment or program with an ordinary one or with a second innovative one. The other strategy is to switch the experimental and control groups at an appropriate point in the experiment, a method which sometimes has advantages from the standpoint of design as well. If a program of remedial reading is being tested, for example, the children in the experimental group for the first six months may then become the control group, and vice versa.

There are a number of rational arguments that the evaluation researcher uses in trying to sell an evaluation study to the practitioners who necessarily must be involved and to the policy makers whose institutions or clients usually constitute the subjects. First, there are rarely, in any community, sufficient resources to provide the kinds of treatment one wishes everyone. Second, it is quite clear, particularly in the prevention and rehabilitation of social ills, that much of current practice is not successful. Only through evaluation research is it possible to sharpen the views and criticisms which policy makers and ordinary citizens should have of the current programs.

The Balance Between Rigor and Reality. The remarks offered on the design of experiments should alert the reader to the need to approximate, as closely as possible, the design of experiments as they are conducted under laboratory conditions. At the same time, the investigator cannot be blind to the constraints placed on his investigations by the realities of the environment in which he conducts his research. Every evaluation experiment should be appraised to ascertain whether the compromises necessary for its conduct are so severe that it would be inadvisable to pursue the research. The answer is rarely unequivocal. It is incumbent on the researcher to inquire, each time, whether the results of the study will be sufficient, or whether arguments which contradict the results could vitiate the usefulness of the research. If the answer is that persuasive arguments can successfully be brought against the research, the policy researcher is well advised to turn his efforts elsewhere. Doing so may raise problems for him, however. As we have noted, many funding agencies now require evaluations of the treatment programs they support. The pressure to undertake evaluation studies merely to conform to these requirements, even when they cannot be well executed, is sometimes formidable. The policy researcher must be aware of these pressures and must not allow them, even subtly, to influence his judgment about whether to embark upon an experiment.

Concluding Comment

Our review of the major research approaches is, of course, by no means complete, as the reader must be aware from the scope of the references we have cited. Many methodological and tactical points have been extensively elaborated upon in the literature. We have merely attempted to indicate the relevance of the different approaches and point out some of the special considerations involved in using them in policy research.

Chapter 7

THE ANALYSIS OF DATA

In social-policy research, as in all research, data are gathered for a purpose. Explicity or implicitly, there is a study design which outlines what data are to be obtained, how, and the way they are to be analyzed in order to answer the set of questions which initiated the enquiry. Within the framework of this book, research questions may be grouped under three headings: description; prediction; and causal analysis. In each instance, the question-answering process is one of inference. The notion of inference simply summarizes the fact that the general purpose of enquiry is to permit conclusions—conclusions based on evidence and logic. These conclusions are communicated in the form of statements—descriptive, predictive, or causal. Two important aspects of the process of making inferences should be noted: (1) the statements that can or should be made about the particular sample studied; and (2) the extent to which the study permits statements to be made beyond the sample actually studied. The latter issue is usually referred to as the problem of *generalization*.

The Problems of Inference

The two problems of inference may be thought of as the internal and external validity of the findings. *Internal validity* is the extent to which one may have confidence in the applicability of the findings to the sample studied. *External* validity is the extent to which one may confidently apply the findings to populations beyond the sample actually studied. To generalize on the basis of evidence is, of course, the very essence of science. But it should be readily apparent that unless one can have confidence in the internal validity of the findings, there is no point at all in even considering their external validity. The results of descriptive, predictive, and experimental investigations are scientifically and practically valuable only to the extent that the findings can be generalized beyond the persons studied, but confidence in making statements about *them* is a prerequisite.

Problems of inference are reduced by designs which include statements of the alternative results and conclusions that can be made, given a particular outcome. This is not typically done in sociological studies, however, in part because of our primitive level of knowledge of social behavior and social relations; moreover, most designs include so many variables that the task of explicating the alternative inferences, is rendered too laborious (Lazarsfeld and Rosenberg, 1955).

Most commonly, the inferential process takes place concomitantly with data analysis. In the majority of studies, although the researcher may have set forth the desired order of analysis at the beginning, he develops the more subtle aspects of his analytic procedures as he reviews his data. Data analysis can be thought of as a process in which one constantly seeks to sharpen and refine one's inferences. A number of special considerations need, therefore, to be reviewed here, primarily because the risks of the overextension as well as the underextension of inferences are major problems to the responsible researcher.

Assuming we have confidence about the internal validity, external validity is essentially a problem of sampling. The proper procedures for selecting samples are well covered in a variety of volumes (e.g., Kish, 1965). From the technical standpoint, sampling is an effort to obtain, economically, a representative cross-section of a population, i.e., one that allows the investigator to generalize his results to the population from which the sample is drawn. The degree of confidence the investigator has in generalizing depends upon the likelihood that repeated samplings from the same population would yield similar results. Statistical measures which estimate that probability are well developed. Sampling is a highly sophisticated field of statistics, and most investigators, except when undertaking studies that require the simplest samples, find it necessary to consult with a sampling expert.

Sampling and Generalization. The important relationship between the sample and the possibility of external validity of the findings can be illustrated by a simple example. Assume that a group of men and women have been carefully and repeatedly weighed within a short period of time on an expensive, thoroughly tested, and inspected scale. The internal validity of such a study would be very high. The measurements of the weights of the members of the study group at that time would be highly reliable, precise, and accurate. Similarly reliable, precise, and accurate estimates of the differences between the mean weights of the men and the women, as subgroups of the studied sample, could also be produced. But if the sample had been haphazardly or simply conveniently selected—the men and women at the local Firemen's Ball, for example—the findings would have virtually zero external validity, even for the general population of firemen and their female dance-hall companions.

The relationship between external and internal validity should be re-emphasized. Much, if not all, of our discussion of data-gathering procedures in the preceding chapters assumed the basic prerequisite of internal validity, namely, sound data. This is a logical and practical starting place. For, although there is a sense in which the procedures for establishing internal and external validity are independent—that is, it is theoretically possible to gather hopelessly invalid, unreliable, and inaccurate data about a perfectly drawn sample—it would seem to be obviously useless and perhaps even dangerous to generalize nonsense.

The Extension of Findings. Many of the studies from which inferences are drawn about social behavior and social processes in the United States have been made in single locations, and of selected populations. Notions about the relationship of social class to mental illness, for example, have become widespread because of Hollingshead and Redlich's (1958) study of New Haven; ideas about the behavior of lower-class, older adolescents are usually drawn from Whyte's (1955) study of boys in the North End of Boston; and key notions about the quality of medical care stem from Peterson's (1956) investigation of North Carolina physicians. The policy researcher, particularly as an advisor to policy makers, must take the findings of completed investigations and generalize from one population to another, but it is important that he explicitly acknowledge the possible limitations in generalizing from a particular study.

There are no hard-and-fast rules about when one does and does not generalize. The point to be made is: the greater the discrepancies between the studied population and a second one, in the characteristics believed to influence the findings, the less likely it is that the results can be generalized from one to the other. Sometimes measures of characteristics of study groups are available because there is information about the population from which they are drawn. In the example given, of a delinquency-prevention program, there would be considerable information in the census about the areas where the boys lived. This would be useful in considering generalizing the findings to a new group. Ordinarily, however, it is necessary to obtain fresh, additional information so that the study group can be described well.

All too often investigators fail to give careful enough consideration to which characteristics of their study group are most relevant. Thus, they fall back on the traditions of their field. Sociologists, for example, often describe their study groups in terms of age, sex, socioeconomic status, marital status and so on, yet they hardly ever describe any physical characteristics of their populations even when these may be relevant. In policy research, an adequate profile is all-important, since one of the intentions of much of the work is to provide the policy maker with results on which he can base decisions. The cost of programs and the limitation of resources require that there be a careful inspection of the similarities between the groups which have been studied and the populations to which the investigator wishes to generalize.

If generalization is the objective, sampling is a key issue no matter which data-gathering approach is used—surveys, records, case studies, field studies, or experiments. It should also be readily apparent that the question of external validity, and therefore sampling, is also pertinent no matter which of the basic research goals the study has—description, prediction, or causal analysis. The task may be to estimate the number of people in a given community who have diabetes, to describe the characteristics of school dropouts, to predict the future use of a community service, or to estimate the effect of a remedial reading program on the reading or general academic performance of retarded readers. In each case, assuming internal validity, the question still remains of whether anything can be said beyond the facts learned about the cases studied. For example, given the obtained rate of prevalence of diabetes among the sample studied, can a confident estimate be made of the prevalence of diabetes in the community?

Predictive Analysis

Prediction is a form of generalization which has a number of different meanings—weather forecasting, theoretical physics, and statistical regression analysis, for example. Their common theme, however, is basic: can something be said about one set of phenomena on the basis of information about one or more other sets of phenomena? To take a relatively simple example, consider the kinds of questions that might be asked of his policy researcher by the administrator of a city hospital.

He might ask, on the one hand, What are the characteristics of the people using the hospital's services? He might also ask, What predictions about future demand for the hospital's services can be made? Both questions have a predictive aspect, although in the first case it is implicit. Presumably, the administrator does not regard the answer to his question as a matter of historical interest; there is an assumption that the answer will describe future patients in his hospital, at least in the near future. The assumption is that current or past users are representative of a broader, unstudied population of future users—often a very shaky assumption, by the way. But once the assumption is made, the process of inferring the answer is no different than when, to use a previous example, an estimate of the number of diabetes cases in a community is made on the basis of a study of a sample of that community. The difference is in the confidence that one can have in the representativeness of the samples, and in the validity of the assumptions upon which the inferences are based.

ASSUMPTIONS FOR POLICY DEVELOPMENT

The fundamental assumption that our hospital administrator has made—and that his policy researcher is making in casting the projection for him—is that there are not going to be any significant changes in the characteristics of the people using the hospital. Lacking the opportunity to improve upon the information available, it is certainly rational for the administrator to plan and act on the basis of what data he has. The study might reveal, for example, that 30 per cent of the hospital's seriously ill patients, but who recover, live alone and have no one to care for them upon release. Upon this information he may base decisions about release policy, the allocation of hospital beds, and the deployment of professional and auxiliary services and personnel.

A somewhat improved procedure would be to make a series of studies over a period of time, with the aim of uncovering any trends in the characteristics of the hospital's clientele. They may be getting younger or older, richer or poorer or, to use the previous example, increasingly fewer or more of them may live alone. Predictions about trends provide for the inclusion of change—in this case, changes in the characteristics of the users of a service. But such predictions are also limited in that they assume the constancy of the conditions or the constancy of the changes in the conditions producing the changes in the clientele.

More sophisticated prediction seeks a constancy in the relationships among the variables, particularly between each of the predictor variables and the variable to be predicted. For example, our administrator really has no basis, in his descriptive study of the characteristics of the people using the hospital, to predict future demand, because he has no information about the relationship between each of the characteristics that has been studied and the use of the hospital. He needs, at a minimum, information about nonusers, and about users of other hospitals. An analysis of trends would provide a basis for predicting future demand, but only on the assumption that no significant changes are taking place in the conditions in the community or in the characteristics of its population which are related to the use of his hospital. Devices which also take into consideration changes in any of the predictor variables should produce more accurate predictions. If, for example, race were an important variable in the equation, a stepped-up rate of change in the racial composition of the community would lead to altered predictions about future demand for the hospital's services.

THE PREDICTION OF FUTURE EVENTS

The distinction between prediction as it is generally treated in statistical analysis and the prediction of future events should perhaps be made at this point. Statistical prediction based on a regression equation describes the functional relationship between one or more predictor, or independent, variables and a criterion, or dependent variable. The question is, How accurately can the values of the dependent variable be predicted on the basis of the other information, the predictor variables? This is, in a sense, prediction without a time dimension: both sets of events, the predictor and the to-be-predicted, have already occurred. The goal is to do better, using additional information, than one can do using information on the dependent variable alone. To take a simple example, if the goal is to "predict" the IQ's of a sample of students (whose IQ's are really already known), other information about the same students would be gathered; these other scores would be regressed against the IQ scores, and the predicted scores would be computed on the basis of the resulting equation. To the extent that there was significantly less error in these predictions than in predictions based on the mean IQ of the sample of students alone, prediction would be judged possible. The less the error in the predictions—in technical terms, the square of the difference between the actual and the "predicted" scores—the better the prediction.

In the prediction of future events, the distribution of scores on the dependent variable are not available beforehand, by definition. Predictions for such a group can only be made on the basis of equations constructed from information about one or more previous samples. These equations are then applied to the new sample, using data about them based on the predictor variables. The assumption now is not that the old and new samples have like characteristics, but that the same relationships among the variables will hold. The accuracy of such predictions can be tested when data about the dependent variable has been obtained. The standard of comparison for these predictions, however, should not be predictions based on the new data about the dependent variable, but on the mean of the old sample.

Causal Analysis

Although semantic and philosophical difficulties surround the notions of description and prediction, they are minor compared with those surrounding the concept of causation. The literature on causation in the philosophy of science abounds with controversy. But however the issue may be defined, or for that matter evaded, there is little doubt that there is a generally prevailing view that the highest form of knowledge is knowledge of a causal nature—something beyond the mere description of facts or even the correlations among variables.

THE CONCEPT OF CAUSATION

Causation is a term used widely both in everyday life and in science. When someone places a lit match near some crumpled newspapers in his fireplace, and the papers burst into flame, the notions of cause and effect seem to be rather obviously demonstrated: the lighted match caused the papers to burn. A slightly more sophisticated everyday analysis would recognize that other factors, particularly the presence of oxygen, were relevant to the process. A scientific explanation of the event would be much more complicated, involving many technical terms and theoretical ideas. But whatever the level of analysis, there seems to be a common underlying theme: a causal factor makes a difference; things would have been different if "it" hadn't been there or if "it" hadn't happened. If we cannot say that "it" invariably makes a difference, then there must be at least a sufficiently high *probability* that it did or will make a difference.

Viewed in this way, the basic problem is: how do we know when something has made a difference in something else? Rather cogent and persuasive arguments have been advanced for the position that we have causal knowledge when we can base accurate predictions on it. But this approach would appear to be satisfactory only if certain restrictions are placed upon the kinds of predictions which are to be regarded as representing evidence of causal knowledge. For one thing, simple statistical relationships among variables must be ruled out as sufficient evidence, in themselves, of causal connections, although, as subsequent discussion will reveal, they may be the starting point of causal analyses. What we require, then, are some rules for deciding the extent to which the evidence indicates that something made a difference and, ideally, how much of a difference it made. Following is a brief introduction to a few old and a few relatively new approaches to this problem.

THE CAUSAL ANALYSIS OF NONEXPERIMENTAL DATA

Given the lack of opportunity for experimentation, it is often necessary to approximate, in nonexperimental analysis, the equivalent of experimental controls. This is usually done with survey data of one type or another. A variety of statistical procedures makes it possible to "partial out" irrelevant or contaminating variables while studying the relationship of one or more independent variables to a dependent one. Such statistical analyses have their analogs in qualitative studies; there, the researcher must either take other potentially explanatory variables into account when he selects his cases or try to marshal enough persuasive evidence against other explanations and for his own. In general, social researchers agree that, at best, these types of analyses can yield only quasi-causal explanations. But since there is little prospect for experiments in many areas, tentative inferences of a causal type, based on nonexperimental studies, are essential (see Wilkins, 1969, particularly chaps. 9–11).

There are various ways of undertaking a quasi-causal analysis (Lazarsfeld and Rosenberg, 1955; Blalock, 1964; Duncan, Haller, and Portes, 1968). A full discussion of the different approaches would involve a great deal of technical material; we can, however, undertake some general discussion of several approaches that are widely used in quasi-causal studies.

MATCHING VS. STATISTICAL CONTROLS

Because of the restriction on opportunities for randomization and because of the difficulty of maintaining intact study groups, it is often necessary to develop much larger study populations than are needed simply for statistical evaluation. Moreover, the researcher normally must compromise, employing procedures of one sort or another in order to establish comparable groups.

In the past, procedures for controlling comparability were commonly derived from *matching,* in which those characteristics that were thought to be contaminations were accounted for by making sure that they were equalized in the experimental and control groups.

Matching can be undertaken before or after the research is done, and may be on either a group or individual basis. The choice of the variables to be matched should be based either on knowledge of the other influences which might affect the experimental variable or on a correlational analysis which identifies correlates of the dependent variable within the study group. For example, in the Highfields study, the investigators developed a prediction table on which scores for a variety of factors, such as the city of residence and skin color, were entered. Boys with similar scores were then compared in order to determine the efficacy of programs (Freeman and Weeks, 1956).

In many cases, matching is badly done, in the sense that there is limited evidence that the factors being matched are the most relevant ones. Moreover, they may not in themselves be a sufficient explanation for the variations in outcome. Incomplete or poor matching is related to the fact that some researchers are not creative in selecting variables. It is also related to the difficulty of matching well, on an individual basis a wide variety of characteristics.

Matching of groups, the goal being to have entire groups be equal, is less difficult. One is interested only in marginal totals; thus, the characteristics of individuals may vary from the experimental to the control group. The differences between group and individual matching are indicated in Table 7.1.

TABLE 7.1

Difference between Individual and Group Matching

	Individual Matching		Group Matching	
	Experimental Group	Control Group	Experimental Group	Control Group
a	White, 16, Parents divorced	White, 16, Parents divorced	White, 16, Parents divorced	White, 14, Parents divorced
b	White, 14, Parents married	White, 14, Parents married	White, 14, Parents married	Negro, 15, Parents married
c	White, 15, Parents separated	White, 15, Parents separated	White, 15, Parents separated	White, 15, Parents separated
d	Negro, 15, Parents married	Negro, 15, Parents married	Negro, 15, Parents married	White, 16, Parents married

In both cases, the control and experimental samples are the same. Each contains three white boys and one Negro, two boys aged 15 and two aged 14 and 16, of one divorced, one separated, and two married sets of parents. In individual matching, each matched set of boys has the same characteristics. In group matching, the over-all picture is the same because of the sum total of the characteristics, without the individual boys being alike. The individual matching procedure has the advantage of taking into account the combined influence of different factors, but it may be more difficult to accomplish. Group matching is easier, but does not take into account the possibility that the simultaneous presence of different characteristics may alter their single effects (what is referred to, technically, as "interaction effects").

The choice between the two depends upon the number of variables considered important enough to take into account as well as upon the availability of cases. When matching takes place before data collection, individual matching of cases or variables is usually attempted. This is ideally done on the basis of descriptive studies from which we can estimate the risk of not finding cases. Often, the matching is done after data collection, to develop comparable groups *ex post facto:* then, individual matching is usually hard to accomplish. Sometimes a combination of individual and group matching is undertaken, the variables deemed most critical being individually matched, and group matching being used for those regarded as of less relevance.

Matching is only valuable if the variables matched constitute the key contaminations or other determinants of the link between independent and dependent variables, but evidence to show which are the key determinants is often not available. It is often impossible, in any event, to match all the variables believed to be pertinent. However, generalizations are limited to matched cases only, and findings are therefore inapplicable to mismatched ones. *Randomization is clearly desirable, whenever possible.*

ANALYSIS OF COVARIANCE

In recent years, matching often has been supplanted by analyses of covariance (Edwards, 1962). Innovations in techniques of covariance analysis, as well as the availability of computers, have advanced the use of statistical examination of questions of contamination. The analysis of covariance makes feasible the simultaneous control of a large number of variables while the relationships between the intervention and the outcome variables are being observed. However, the analysis of covariance, though probably far superior to matching, does require a fair degree of sophistication in statistical analysis and, to save labor, a computer. In many cases researchers require statistical consultation because of the complexities of covariance analysis and the many alternative adjustments available.

As we have said, the analysis of covariance is a procedure for simultaneously taking into account variables that may contaminate the relationship between the independent and dependent measures. The procedure allows for "adjusting" the relationship for one variable or for many, through the use of introduced adjusters which compensate for *a priori* differences between the groups designated as experimental or control, or who are receiving different treatment. It is analogous to other procedures for taking out contaminating effects, but it is the most valuable one because it provides a means of separately adjusting the various groups involved in the study. Covariance procedures are still being refined and computer programs are being developed (Jones, forthcoming).

Some statisticians prefer the use of partial and multiple correlation techniques rather than covariance procedures (Cohen, 1968). Like covariance analysis, these correlation procedures involve examining the relationship between two variables while taking into account the influence of one or more additional variables (Blalock, 1964). This approach too involves quite complex statistical procedures, usually undertaken only when high-speed computers are available. The virtues of correlation analyses in comparison with covariance procedures rest on arguments far too complex to even be summarized here, although it is fair to say that some of the leaders in psychological measurement are strong advocates of a correlation approach. Needless to note, either technique is preferable to ignoring the possible influence of variables on the relationship between the independent and dependent ones.

THE TEST VARIABLE

The test variable is an idea closely associated with the work of Lazarsfeld and Rosenberg (1955). Their approach requires the investigator to repeatedly introduce additional variables into the analysis, as a test, to see whether the presumed causal relationship still will continue to hold. As an illustration, one might find a relationship between reading newspapers and voting Republican. Does the reading of newspapers cause one to vote Republican? Test variables might include income, since income may be related to the purchasing of newspapers, or education, since people with more education may read more, or other variables that might explain away the original finding. If income is the test variable, the sample of community members who had been interviewed concerning newspaper reading and political party affiliation would be studied by income level. If income was not known, a new study would have to be done in which income data as well as the other information would be collected. The analysis would consist of examining the association between reading newspapers and voting Republican among persons of high, moderate, and low income. If the finding were the same for each of the income groups, income would be discarded as a test variable and another one would be introduced.

It is possible, of course, to introduce combinations of variables. It is also possible to expand the original notion by associating several independent variables with a dependent variable, or by introducing indexes made up of a number of variables.

THE INTERACTION APPROACH

Numerous methods exist for studying the relationships of three or more variables simultaneously. Most of the highly sophisticated methods require that the variables be ordered ones, preferably measurements along a scale. Even for data in the form of attributes, such as skin color and sex, there are techniques which enable us to study the interactive effects of at least three variables (Goodman, 1965).

The interaction approach is somewhat different from the test-variable one. The question now is: if the influence of a varible on two others is removed, what does it do to the relationship between the remaining two variables? If the relationship becomes much weaker or disappears, one may presume that it was due to the influence of the removed variable. If it remains the same or becomes stronger, then one may presume that the third variable made no difference or even masked part of the influence of the first variable upon the second; in that case, it could be presumed that, if the third variable is randomly distributed, the relationship between the other two would be found. One could then hypothesize that there is a causal link between the two variables.

Perhaps an example will make the approach clearer. Let us say that a correlation is found between income and feelings of happiness, and that a relationship exists between education and income, and between education and feelings of happiness. If you simultaneously try to take into account the last two relationships, what happens to the relationship between income and feeling happy? If it holds, or improves, when the relationships between education and these two variables is taken into account, there is some plausibility to the notion of a causal sequence.

PATH ANALYSIS

Path analysis is a correlational approach in which the investigator develops a model, or rather, chooses from a series of models the one which best explains the relationship between two variables. Through path analysis, an effort is made to understand the correlation between two variables. The approach entails including, within the model, hypothetical values for "dummy" variables or values not measured. These are derived from alternative views as to the interaction of the morass of variables. Path analysis is employed in order to develop what appears to be a rational causal sequence (Duncan, 1966; Duncan, Hiller, and Portes, 1968). Although it is impossible to explain the notion further here, the reader should be aware of the promise which models and path analysis hold for certain types of studies.

The Analysis of Experimental Data

The basic inferences which can properly be made from experimental data are largely determined by the design and conduct of the investigation. It can be said that the basic task of experimental design is to produce estimates of the *true* effects of experimental treatments (or interventions) which are as precise as possible. The emphasis is on "true" effects, as compared with observed or apparent effects, because of the problems of error. The emphasis is also on precision, because of the problems of error in statistical inference. The adequate analysis of experimental data requires that the total experiment be reviewed in an effort to reveal flaws in the experiment which might account for the findings which emerged—whether positive or negatively related to the intervention hypothesis. That is, are there other plausible hypotheses which might account for some of the findings, and to what extent were these other hypotheses ruled out by the design or conduct of the experiment? There are some standard "other" hypotheses which are (or, at least, should be) examined.

AN ILLUSTRATION OF AN EXPERIMENT

Suppose we have designed and executed an experimental program in which we attempt, through a house-to-house educational campaign, to improve the nutritional content of family meals. Suppose that our experiment also includes an effort to compare the effectiveness of two different educational programs.

A population of families would be identified, and three random samples would be selected from that population. One randomly selected sample would be exposed to Program 1—consisting, let us say, of face-to-face discussion and persuasion as well as printed instructional material. The second sample would be exposed to Program 2—consisting of the content of Program 1 plus actual demonstrations in the home. The third sample would be exposed to neither program, thus constituting the control group for the experiment. Subsequently, after the experimental groups had been exposed to the program, the nutritional content of the meals served by all the families would be measured. The basic research questions might be: (1) Can the nutritional content of family meals be improved by a house-to-house educational program? and (2) Do the two programs have different effects?

Let us assume that the findings show that there are statistically significant differences among the criterion measures (the nutritional content of meals after the program) for the three groups, Group 2 having a significantly higher average score than the control group. Now we must analyze those findings.

The focus of the analysis of experimental data is on the variation in the criterion, or the dependent variable, within the total study population—i.e., on total variance. There will almost certainly be variation *within each group*—that is, differences among the scores of the members of each group considered separately—, and there may be variation *among the average scores of the experimental and control groups*. The total variance, the differences among the scores of *all* the members of the study population considered as one group, may be due to a number of different factors or sources. A properly designed experiment provides a basis for analyzing the total variance into a number of possible sources of variation.

When the study population is considered as one group, there will undoubtedly be variation in the criterion, the nutrition scores. This variance (the total variance) may in part be due to the experimental stimuli that was our hypothesis. It is also due, entirely or in part, to random variations in the many other factors which affect the nutritional content of family meals—income, education, attitudes, previous information about nutrition, cultural background, and so on. Some of it may, and probably is, due to errors of measurement, fallible procedures for measuring the nutritional content of family meals. And some of it may be due to flaws in the conduct of the over-all experiment, particularly in the conduct of the different interventions.

The *observed* effects of the experimental programs are the measured differences among the experimental and control groups, i.e., the treatment variance. The significance of those differences is tested by comparing the treatment variance with the variance within the study groups, i.e., the error variance. The fundamental question being asked is, What is the probability that the observed differences among the experimental and control groups can be attributed to chance—that is, to the random draw by which the families were allocated to the three study groups? The statistical assumption is made that the observed differences are chance differences resulting from the randomization process, that the programs had no effect. The evidence is then examined in the light of this hypothesis, known as the null hypothesis, and a new question is asked: How often would differences as great as these be likely to occur by chance? The answer to this question, provided by relating the data to a previously chosen probability or significance level, forms the basis for the decision to accept or reject the null hypothesis. As we noted earlier, this test of significance consists primarily of a comparison of the treatment variance (a function of the differences among the means of the groups) and the error variance (the variance within the groups). The technique is quite appropriately called the analysis of variance. The statistics are usually done on a computor, here we are concerned with the principles involved.

Within the limits of chance, the randomization process thus allows the experimenter to deal mathematically with the probably large number of uncontrolled factors, known and unknown, which affect the nutritional content of family meals. However, it should be apparent that the magnitude of the variance within groups is related to the number and influence of such factors. And since the *significance* of observed differences is a function of the error within groups, the error variance, it is important in experimental design to attempt to minimize the error variance. One technique, sometimes referred to as the randomized-block design, involves grouping experimental subjects into units or blocks. The assumption, usually based on previously acquired knowledge, is that the members within each block will be more homogeneous with respect to the criterion variable. In the analysis of variance, the differences between blocks (the between-blocks variance) will be subtracted from the error variance before the significance of the findings is calculated.

The point of our discussion and of our example is that statistical inference regarding the significance of observed differences among means on our criterion scores involved two kinds of error—commonly referred to in the literature as Type 1 and Type 2 error. *Type 1 error* occurs when a true null hypothesis is rejected as false; that is, in the case of inferences about experimental effects, when the decision is made that effects have occurred when they have not. *Type 2 error* occurs when a false null hypothesis has been accepted as true; that is, in the case of inferences about experimental effects, when the decision is made that effects have not occurred when they have.

The risk of Type 1 error can be reduced by setting a more stringent level of statistical significance, but unfortunately, this increases the risk of Type 2 error. The risk of Type 2 error depends on: (1) the magnitude of the true effects of the interventions; and (2) the precision of the experiment. And since the precision of an experiment depends upon the error variance and the size of the study groups, experiments should be based upon informed estimates of error variance and upon judgments about how large an effect the experimenter is willing to regard statistically as chance. Once the acceptable levels of risk of Type 1 and Type 2 errors have been specified, the minimum size of the study groups required can be stated.

SAMPLING ERROR

The kind of error we have been dealing with is *sampling error,* sometimes referred to as "subjects' error" (Lindquist, 1956). Another kind of sampling error which might intrude upon the findings of an experiment such as our nutritional education experiment arises from the allocation of program or intervention personnel to the two experimental groups. If, for example, more enthusiastic or skilled people were assigned to one of the educational programs, we might attribute the observed effects to differences in the programs when they are actually due to differences in the personnel. In addition to careful training and supervision of personnel and monitoring of the conduct of the program, randomization of personnel constitutes the main defense against the intrusion of this kind of error.

Another source of error is *measurement error,* arising from the lack of reliability of the estimates of the criterion variable. As we observed earlier, measurement errors include *random error* and *bias*. If it is possible to obtain a large number of measurements for the same individual, the average score of these measurements ordinarily will approach a limit as the number of measurements is increased. The assumed reason is that the random errors of measurement are being averaged out. If there is no bias in the estimates, this limit is the *true value*. In the estimation of the effects of experimental interventions, random error may be more of a methodological problem than bias, if the bias is constant throughout the measurement procedures. Random error is a fundamental problem, because we seldom have the opportunity to obtain large numbers of measures and estimates of a subject's score and are thus more likely to base to be measured, and the assignment of measures as well, be randomized in order to have any confidence in the results.

In the nutrition experiment, for example, the estimate of the nutritional content of a family's meals would ideally be based on a large number of randomly selected, carefully measured meals. In practice, only one or a few such measures, probably not randomly selected, would be used. Under such circumstances, measurement error might be responsible for a large part or even all of the observed differences. If repeated measures cannot be made, it is imperative that the selection of the particular meals to be measured, and the assignment of measurers as well, be randomized.

In short, the analysis of experimental data must include the consideration of evidence, presented or available, of the reliability of the estimates obtained by the measuring procedures used. These considerations should include: information concerning other, prior, uses of the same procedures or instruments; carefulness of the administration of the procedures; the availability of repeated measures of the same subjects; the use of two or more sets of procedures to measure the same phenomenon; and the size of the population measured.

The basic error which a lack of *validity* in the measuring procedures would introduce is almost too obvious to mention. If the estimates obtained are not of the nutritional content of meals but of something else, clearly any conclusions about the effects of the programs on the nutritional content of meals are unwarranted. It should also be clear that, even if experimental effects appear to have occurred, great caution should be exercised in making inferences beyond these findings to presumed or possible more far-reaching consequences of these effects. For example, it should not be assumed—except perhaps on the basis of evidence obtained outside of this experiment—that the experiment had an effect on the nutritional content of the food actually eaten by the experimental families or on the nutritional benefit obtained therefrom.

The Hawthorne Effect

One problem of causal inference is related to inability to separate out specific elements of a program in establishing the efficacy of inputs. The notion, perhaps over-used, that doing anything has an impact, originated in the Western Electric research described in Chapter 2. It has been suggested, for example, that the supposed efficacy of tranquilizers in curtailing symptoms of mental illness is not due to the drugs themselves but to the phenomenon of nurses, physicians and ward attendants feeling that the patients are going to do better and thus behaving differently towards them (Freeman and Simmons, 1960). In other words, some researchers believe that different expectations lead the staff into different types of relationships with the patients and that in consequence, their symptoms are partially alleviated. Evidence of a related type comes from Rosenthal's (1968) study which indicated that students randomly labeled "smart" do better in the classroom.

In order to overcome the Hawthorne Effect, several studies of the impact of tranquilizers have used what is referred to as a "double-blind" approach (Klerman, 1966). In such studies placebos are employed for a control group, and neither the patients nor the staff (except one member who does not see the patients) have any knowledge of which patients are receiving tranquilizers and which patients are not. In the event that severe symptomatology requires a regimen of exceptional treatment, the patient can be withdrawn from the experiment.

The double-blind procedure is only one way to minimize experimenter contamination. Another is to have a number of different groups in the experiment, in order to isolate the impact of extraneous inputs. The design of a study of the impact of nutrition on mental and social development called for providing food twice a day to all the children in small Guatemalan villages. This being the case, not only were the children receiving food, but food handlers came into the villages and both the children and their parents thus had expanded interpersonal contacts. In order to examine whether it was truly the food that had the impact, or the contacts, a second experimental setting was recommended. In a second setting, efforts were made, in the guise of health education, to have the same extent of contact between villagers and persons from the outside.

There is a vast and a growing body of literature on experimental design, and a host of techniques not only for improving the sensitivity of experiments and the precision of the estimates of the effects, but also to enable the experimenter to obtain simultaneous estimates of the effects of more than one stimulus and the interactions among the multiple stimuli as well (Edwards, 1967; Cochran and Cox, 1950). Earlier, we pointed out that opportunities to conduct, in the real world, social experiments that are consistent with the canons of social research are extremely rare, and it clearly will be quite a while before there are many opportunities to use some of the more powerful and elaborate types of designs that are being developed. But a growing exception to this statement is the potential applicability of experimental designs in the evaluation of the effects of programs and practices in health, education, and welfare.

THE IMPORTANCE OF DIFFERENCES

There is a difference between what is significant from a technical standpoint and what is significant from a practical one. The issue can be viewed most clearly in terms of quantitative data. In dealing with data of a quantitative nature, like percentages, mean or average values, or the degree of association between variables, the traditional practice has been to apply tests of significance. The concept of tests of significance is commonly used in sample studies in order to estimate the true distribution of variables, a *true distribution* being the extent to which measures of central tendency or of proportions are stable, or to which variation can be expected around the particular value because of sampling error. Such tests of significance permit us to judge the likelihood that replication will yield noncontradictory results. Thus, when one sees in reports such notations as "p is less than .05, chi-square test," the figures refer to the association of one variable with another. That "p is less than .05" indicates that in less than 5 per cent of the cases is it likely that differences revealed by the association of one variable with another will be chance ones and that, at least 95 times out of 100, the result of a replication would be the same.

Within social research there are controversies about the application of tests of significance (see, e.g., Gold, 1969; Duggan and Dean, 1968). First of all, the confidence limit varies. Psychologists, for instance, ordinarily tend to work at the .01 per cent level; and sociologists, at the .05 per cent level. Some argue that, as fields become more developed, it is fair to use a narrower confidence limit; others maintain that the matter is of little consequence except when the decisions based upon the findings are crucial, involving, for example, the risk of life. Some hold that any arbitrary level is incorrect, rather that the confidence level should always be stated so all may evaluate the finding.

Academic researchers, in general, veer towards the conservative side. If there is any bias, it is normally on unwillingness to reject a true null hypothesis and a willingness to accept a false one: that is, we probably disguise more findings than we should. At times this conservatism is criticized by field personnel. The policy-oriented researcher should think through this type of problem carefully, for his orientation is somewhat different. Rather than using the traditional confidence limits in his field as his yardstick, he must estimate on a study-by-study basis. In fields where there is little knowledge of the results of intervention and the particular intervention proposed cannot be construed as seriously detrimental to the parties concerned, policy makers should be extremely liberal. In areas where there are a number of alternative strategies available and where a new intervention may create danger to the subjects, a conservative approach should be employed.

Statistical significance, nevertheless, has little to do with practical significance. This point is clear when entire populations are under study, instead of samples. Is there then any reason to use tests of significance? Some investigators argue strongly that there should be. First, in most social investigations, and particularly social-policy ones, the implicit intent is to generalize to other, equivalent types of study populations. This is so even if the original study contains a whole population. If, for example, one has studied all the patients in a particular Veterans Administration hospital, the extension of the findings to similar hospitals is implied. Second, it is argued that the researcher and those concerned with his work must have some formal means of estimating the practical or substantive significance of the findings.

With certain kinds of empirical data, there is an alternative to tests of significance. These are measures of association. Many researchers who are not interested in the over-all problems of statistical significance, but rather with the extent of relationships between measures, substitute a measure of association as a means of evaluation. It is common to see correlation coefficients reported, rather than measures of significance, and an effort is made to discover the utility or the degree of variation that can be explained by the particular association. For example, with a large enough sample, a predictive study may demonstrate a significant correlation between two variables. In fact, however, it may be that perhaps only one per cent of the variance in one variable is explained by the second variable.

For the social-policy researcher, it is true that the use of some consistent level of significance or of some arbitrary degree of magnitude of relationship is valuable. Yet it is not a sufficient safeguard against his unwittingly making different interpretations of similar empirical results. *Practical significance* means more than either formally examining the contents of a study in terms of sampling error or taking steps to insure consistency of interpretation. It also takes into account the nature of the problem. By way of simple illustration, let us presume that, after studying the past performance of horses for ten hours, a man bets $2 on a race and wins $20 (an unlikely occurrence, by the way). Winning the bet might be of practical significance to a man who could earn $1.50 an hour if he chose to work those ten hours, yet not for the man who could earn $50 in those ten hours. In many endeavors, the social-policy researcher is confronted, on an intuitive level, with problems exactly like this.

Practical significance is a key factor in judgments of a descriptive and evaluative character. Crime prevention programs that reduce crimes against persons by 2 per cent may be of more practical significance than programs which reduce petty acts against property by 10 or 15 per cent, for example. The difficulty is to find criteria on which to base estimates of practical significance. Unless there are such criteria, or comparative data, practical decisions become dependent on values. This is why cost-benefit analysis has become popular. While formal programs of cost-benefit analysis employ values, of course (usually dollars), they do enable us to reduce disparate results to a common frame of reference. In the absence of a comparative standard, persuasiveness and the immediate political and social pressures carry the field.

The infant mortality rate illustrates the importance of a comparative estimate. The rate in the United States dropped markedly until the 1960's, but changes since then have been relatively insignificant. Studying the data independently, one might suppose that the comparatively small fluctuations in the infant mortality rate since 1960 are of no practical significance. However, data from the Scandinavian countries continues to show small but regular declines in infant mortality. And if the data from the United States is disaggregated by region or by skin color, one begins to see that the American infant mortality programs are not effective, particularly among low-income groups.

Concluding Comment

In this chapter we have dealt with various methods of research and have indicated the relevance of social-policy research as well as its limitations. Many points could not be fully discussed because of their technical nature; nevertheless, the material should alert the reader to the problems involved in drawing inferences from social-policy research. Inference making is carried on in the context of the given research problem, and involve more than the formal process of testing the acceptability of an hypothesis.

Chapter 8

THE DYNAMICS OF THE SOCIAL RESEARCH TASK

At the start of this volume, we indicated that it is the attitude and him from his peers engaged in social-science research, more than differences in technique. At the outset, it should be noted that there is little material on the way social-policy researchers work. Although, from time to time, accounts of the research role have been provided (Hammond, 1964), the general paucity of information forces our own examination to be highly impressionistic. It derives, for the most part, from the casual observations and experiences of the authors. Other researchers who undertake social-policy studies may disagree with our impressions.

So far, we have emphasized the technical activities of the social-policy researcher. In order for him to do his job well, however, he must be competent in a wide range of other tasks. The technical procedures can be taught in the classroom or gleaned from books, but these interpersonal and nontechnical aspects of the social policy researcher's job are generally learned in the doing. Technical astuteness is in itself insufficient preparation for the conduct of research studies, and certainly insufficient for a successful career in social-policy research. The researcher must recognize the importance of administration, of locating and obtaining financial support, and of developing and maintaining a posture that facilitates the necessary interpersonal relationships with policy makers and practitioners.

Administration

Social-policy researchers rarely work alone. The very nature of the work usually requires a reasonably large staff, one which may include other investigators with high levels of academic training, associates with specific technical skills, and clerical assistants. In an interesting study, Andrews (1964) analyzed the productivity of scientists in different fields who were engaged in administrative activities as well as in their own research. He found that those with administrative responsibilities tend to be *more* productive than those who spend full time at the research bench. The explanation he offered is that the most successful, perhaps the most qualified researchers, are given the most responsibility; thus, a relatively large proportion of their day is spent in administration. It is certainly true that the policy researcher who is valued in a large organization, or the investigator in the university who is simultaneously engaged in a number of major projects, spends a significant, if not large, amount of time in an administrative capacity. It is also fair to observe that many inquiries into social policy fail because of the chaos that accompanies poor administration.

Throughout the academic enterprise and the social-research environment, and despite the need for competent administration of research programs, the administrative role is generally regarded as unimportant in comparison with intellectual and research activities. Many persons literally reject their administrative obligations and fail to learn, even after a number of near disasters, that someone must assume procedural and bureaucratic responsibility. In addition, the collegial ethos of academe, in which democratic decision making is usually emphasized, extends to persons doing research in virtually all settings. Nevertheless, in the day-to-day conduct of research investigations—whether they loathe it or not—investigators must not only provide and accept administrative direction, but also acknowledge the importance of allocating responsibility to persons on the basis of competence.

In some organizations, there is a person who is designated as research administrator. He may or may not be the most senior and experienced investigator; sometimes these assignments are terminous, and other times they involve two individuals (Kaplan, 1959). As Kaplan observes, however, the actual duties and responsibilities of the person who serves as the research administrator varies greatly from one organization to another. Sometimes he is responsible for the control and raising of funds; sometimes he recruits the personnel or sometimes the hiring is done by each investigator or section. These are only illustrations of the variety of definitions of the job, but what are some of the key administrative activities that cannot be overlooked? Perhaps these very ones—budget and personnel—as in any organization.

BUDGETING

The cost of research is exceedingly difficult to estimate. Most funds are expended for manpower—that is, for services rather than goods—and it is difficult, in any organization, to estimate the productivity of creative people. Even when hardware is used, e.g., computers, the estimation of costs is difficult. A simple dictum is that sound administration of research requires the development of a regular mechanism for reporting on the budget, so that the investigator knows his financial situation at frequent and regular intervals (Brunner, 1962). A more problematic aspect of fiscal control is how he tailors his investigation when faced with budgeting problems, and how he limits and restricts work that is marginal to the major focus of the investigation.

About all that can be offered here is the warning that most research projects are overambitious and that overexpenditures during the data-collection phase usually become compounded as one moves into data analysis. It is simply impossible to answer, in a single study, all the worthwhile questions that can be thought up. Particularly social-policy investigations, where there is a commitment to provide results of relevance to policy makers and practitioners, the investigator must recognize that his studies cannot be unlimited in scope.

Perhaps the most difficult problem is raised by side ventures, which sometimes may promise to be as profitable as the actual study being undertaken. It should be noted, however, that while serendipity (Barber, 1959) is a frequently advanced explanation for major discoveries, side ventures are a marvelous excuse for not finishing the work to which the researcher has obligated himself. Every organization and every research project must have somebody who is in a position to say "No," or who limits the amount of resources and manpower for peripheral and marginal activities. At the same time, investigators with administrative responsibilities must recognize that the very people who do research, and the very nature of their activity, require a fair degree of permissiveness. The trick is to strike a balance between a completely laissez-faire situation and an authoritarian environment: being too extreme in the former direction is incompatible with the completion of the work, but moving too far in the other direction will undoubtedly stifle creative effort. Nevertheless, whether investigators like it or not, the amount of the available funds restricts what can be done.

PERSONNEL PRACTICES

Personnel practices in the research area are vague and diffuse, partly because they are modeled after those in universities—which in turn are not exactly prototypes of administratively effective organizations—and partly because it is difficult to judge the basis for rewards and privileges. Most research organizations—except those government positions that come under civil service—have vague salary scales. Nevertheless, research investigators and their staffs are very familiar with the advantages of economic affluence, and they are unlikely to be attracted to or remain in settings that do not compete financially for talent.

The remuneration paid to research investigators is often based on the salary scale of university professors and their staffs. Is this a relevant norm? Many research positions in and out of universities carry neither the tenure of professorships nor their prestige, and many times investigators are supporting themselves with personally obtained grant funds and therefore maintain that they deserve to be rewarded for their entrepreneurship. Finally, some maintain that persons who devote all, or a large proportion, of their time to research work harder than a full-time professor. While the salary standards at universities will continue to provide rough guidelines, particularly for persons in nonacademic situations, it is usually necessary to provide salaries more generous than those that prevail in universities.

The other possible set of salary standards is the scale for practitioners and planners in the organization in which the researcher is employed. While they, too, will continue to influence the financial situation of social-research investigators, the range of professional incomes is so great that they hardly are a useful guide. For example, full-time, salaried physicians may earn $35,000 to $50,000 a year in a medical organization. While most social investigators would be delighted with similar rewards, they hardly expect them. On the other hand, many social-welfare agencies pay professionals less than $10,000 a year, and could not obtain the service of qualified research people on the basis of their salary scale for practitioners.

With respect to this aspect of administration, we should note, however, that the rewards of academic research are now fairly generous and becoming more so. The annual survey published in the *Bulletin of the American Association of University Professors* shows that salaries for full professors in high-quality institutions, when prorated over the full year, are well above $20,000. Certainly senior investigators, who are responsible for large staffs and six-digit budgets, expect at least similar remuneration.

WORKING CONDITIONS

A competitive salary-scale, however, is not the whole of personnel relations. Most researchers who have had academic experience expect considerable freedom about hours of work, opportunities to pursue their personal intellectual interests, and accounting for their time. Many universities, for example, have a formal "one-fifth rule," which allows the professors to undertake consultation and special projects one day per week, and many research settings and university research organizations provide a similar perquisite. One large research organization handles the problem of accountability for time by requiring that their professional staff be in the office at least one hour a day, although it may be any one of the 24 hours.

The climate of a research operation simply cannot be the same as that of the operating units of organizations, at least if it wishes to attract good investigators, hold them, and get the best work out of them. Persons charged with the administration of research activities must communicate the differences in tempo, pace, and how work gets done to the other parts of the organization. Friction often occurs because the different orientations and styles of work are not understood. At the same time, persons who move into social policy research from academic life must recognize that their work habits may require some modification. The need to relate to persons in policy roles and to fit into an organizational structure necessarily means giving up some freedom to decide when and where one works.

STATUS

Perhaps the most troublesome aspect of personnel relations is the matter of status, both within the research group and between it and the other parts of a policy-making organization.

Within the research group, difficulties occur both because of differences in the formal educational achievement of persons, and because of differences in technical knowhow and the value placed upon certain types of knowledge in comparison with others. For most persons in social-science research, the doctorate is the *minimum* academic requirement for a full-fledged investigator, certifying his *complete competence* in the variety of skills required for research work. In the arena of social action and social-policy research, however, many persons with considerably less formal training have occupied and continue to occupy senior posts and have undertaken excellent studies. Conversely, individuals just completing their doctoral training in the social and behavioral sciences are not only novices when it comes to day-to-day research activity, but may also lack certain fundamental technical skills. It is easy to suggest that one's position within a research group should be related to one's competence and past performance, rather than simply to formal education, but it is practically impossible to implement a standard based on performance. There are simply too few criteria that can be used. Perhaps more important, there is an unwillingness on the part of those in the field to forsake the standard of formal education. However, the social-policy researcher should at least be prepared to work in an environment in which formal training may not necessarily be a gauge of the relative worth of the person, and he should try to avoid or at least minimize the rigidities of academic status that are most common in the universities.

Another problem of status among the staff arises because some individuals have invaluable technical skills which command a high price. The market value of a top-notch computer programmer, for example, may be greater than that of an investigator with a doctorate. In any policy-research operation, thus, the organizational chart that shows responsibilities may not reflect salaries, and neither responsibility nor pay might reflect reputation or professional prestige. At the very least, the social-policy researcher must be aware of the potential strain and conflict inherent in the structure of the research group.

The work requirements and job relationships in industrial research and development have been the subject of a variety of studies (e.g., Howton, 1963). Many of these studies have a bearing on policy research. In particular, studies such as Howton's point up the relationship between work and interpersonal relations: One's work assignments condition one's interpersonal relationships. The policy researcher with administrative responsibilities must be aware that the scientist is not like the skilled craftsman, who can simply be assigned a job and expected to do it. In research organizations, it is probably as important for the administrator to concern himself with structuring the interpersonal milieu as with defining and allocating tasks. Unless he can control, or at least guide, the interpersonal relationships of his staff, it is unlikely that an enduring and productive group will be maintained.

Earlier, we observed that the differences in the work patterns of research people and others in an organization is a potential source of conflict. Such conflicts, it can be argued, reflect the underlying differences between the research group and what may be referred to as the "production" components of a policy organization. Again, some of the studies of research and development groups in industry are informative (Howton, 1963). Research persons have been described as organizationally rootless. There are few permanent research operations, and investigators expect to move from project to project, while the others in a policy organization, although they also transfer about, probably have much more continuity of responsibility. The researcher is also strongly dependent upon the ethic of mutual aid. He comes from an academic setting and is oriented toward his colleagues; thus, he expects his skills to be exploited by his associates, whether or not they can reciprocate. This is somewhat less true of persons in the human resources and services fields, who come from administrative backgrounds or who are practitioners. Research persons generally have a rather ambiguous position in organizations, and they are likely to be regarded with uncertainty, if not with mistrust and envy, by those in other parts of the organization. Moreover, the research person himself is concerned about not having a clear-cut niche.

RESEARCH UNITS

In general, when a relatively large number of persons are engaged in related research tasks, an effort is made to mold them into some kind of unit or group: thus have developed research centers in universities, and research departments in governmental and volunteer agencies. There are obvious advantages to the arrangement: it facilitates communication among research persons, and it provides for an economical use of hardware, e.g., punch-card equipment and calculators. But the more separate the research unit and its peculiar environment, the greater the likelihood of strain with other departments of the organization.

Some groups which employ researchers assign them to different parts of the program and have only a limited coordination of their researchers. Some professional schools, medical schools for example, may have one or more social-research positions in a number of different technical departments. A decentralized approach, perhaps, does lessen the likelihood of conflict between the in-group and the out-group, but it also makes it harder for the individual investigator to retain his identity, and it may even be less productive. Again, there are no simple solutions or prescriptions that can be offered. Explicating the matter may, nevertheless, be useful and serve as a warning that the policy researcher, particularly the one with administrative responsibility or some say-so as to how the research staff is to be organized, must develop a rationale for the structuring of research personnel within the larger organization.

Control of the Environment

In the discussion of the participation of the researcher in planning, developing, and evaluating programs, we stressed the necessity for him to relate to the range of individuals who serve as policy makers or who are key practitioners. It was emphasized that only through such engagements can the social-policy researcher become and remain, orientated to his tasks. Unless he develops those relationships, he is unlikely to be able to undertake his work without finding barriers of various sorts in his way. In order for the social-policy researcher to prosper in his environment, he needs to achieve a particular posture, both in his own work and toward others.

CLARIFYING WORKING ASSIGNMENTS

An essential component of the social-policy researcher's posture must be an explicit commitment not to needlessly hinder the ongoing activities of the setting in which he is involved. It is important that he not become a rallying point for the dissatisfied and a source of anxiety to others. At the same time, he must not get bogged down in meaningless, piddling administrative and practical tasks, and it is important that practitioners and policy makers recognize and appreciate the uniqueness of his role and contribution.

How does this come about? In part, the researcher's control of the environment requires that he be wise enough to obtain initial agreement about the scope of his work, what the organization may expect of him, and what he expects from his associates. Researchers often enter into ambiguous roles in policy organizations, particularly the inexperienced researcher, who has not yet learned how to interact with the variety of policy makers and practitioners present in most settings.

Clarity is also required about many other administrative matters—budget, staff appointments, opportunities for teaching and consultation, attendance at professional and scientific meetings, and so on. (The need for such clarity is one of the reasons we discussed administration at the outset of this chapter.) The policy researcher must know what is expected of him and to whom he reports. It is inevitable that problems requiring arbitration and decision will arise between persons involved in research and those engaged in the other aspects of policy making and social action.

In many other kinds of research, certainly traditional academic research, researchers are not accountable to a large extent to anyone for what they do as investigators—although, of course, faculty members may be denied tenure or promotion because of a failure to publish. And we have already noted other differences between social-policy settings and typical academic environments. The point here is that social scientists engaged in full-time careers in policy research find themselves almost always in a line-staff organization, and must therefore seek formal assurance that they are not so boxed in that they are prevented from carrying out their tasks.

There are many different ways of carving out a place for oneself, none of which work perfectly. Some policy researchers have available to them a subcommittee of the executive staff or the board of their agency. Others have a technical advisory committee of outside persons, usually research-trained, who guide them on technical and on policy issues. Still others have a panel of consultants who may advise on broad general issues, and who usually advise on the day-to-day conduct of the work. Still others call on *ad hoc* consultants when they need them. Some persons make use of a combination of these approaches. The solutions, as you can see, involve the creation of a mechanism for avoiding having the work restricted by the organizational table.

RELATIONSHIPS TO COLLEAGUES

Many persons in social-policy bodies have previously worked with or have friendly relationships with individuals in the various academic disciplines from whch policy researchers are drawn. Often, therefore, the policy researcher's status, as well as his professional accomplishments, gain him the respect he needs from individuals on the job. Thus, it is not only for his own professional development that informal interaction, contributions to the literature of his discipline, and participation in the affairs of his professional associations are useful; it also is another means of influencing the bodies with whom he works so that they will cooperate and collaborate with him, both because of who he is and the way they perceive him.

Persons in policy-research are well advised not to forsake opportunities to keep one foot in the discipline with which they identify. This advice is easier to give than follow, however. While the academic who engages in policy research often finds himself in an advantageous position, for he has a ready-made reference and membership group, those who turn full time to policy research often face intellectual isolation—and this is not easy to overcome. The maintenance of an identity and visibility among his peers in his discipline is a useful means of controlling his environment.

Finally, it should be noted that policy researchers often find it necessary to develop a much broader substantive and methodological outlook than their academic peers. Not only do they have to learn the approaches and terminology of practitioners, they also often find themselves using a wider range of research procedures than they otherwise might. They may also find that their research group, if they do have colleagues, cuts across disciplinary lines. Again, their problem is one of balance. It is possible to become so eclectic that one cannot maintain one's expertise in one's own area; but if one's interests are too narrow, opportunities as a policy researcher are limited and ability to control the environment is hindered.

At several places in this volume, we have indicated that the development of social policy and the planning of a social program are an outcome of a political process rather than of a formalized, systematic procedure. Manipulative, interpersonal skills are organizationally valuable to the social policy researcher in whatever he does. The very political character of policy making suggests that the investigator who has nurtured a political sense, and who is a "good operator," is indeed fortunate. While no techniques for gaining political competence can be offered here, the point definitely merits notice.

The Concept of Support

In an earlier section of this volume, we indicated that there is a wide-scale recognition, in the health, education, and welfare fields, of the importance of serious policy research. Its conduct, however, requires financial and organizational support.

FINANCIAL SUPPORT

The social-policy researcher is afforded considerable opportunity for launching studies and investigations which require extensive financial support—more so than his colleagues, for there is still relatively limited funding of basic research.

Nevertheless, financial support is not automatically available, and "grantsmanship," though it may seem invidious to some, is of crucial importance to the social-policy researcher. Most of his work entails a relationship with one of a large number of granting agencies. These include, first of all, the many branches of the federal government which, through legislative stipulation, have the authority to provide research funds. There are also private foundations which have entered the policy-research arena, sometimes with magnificent research support. Finally, operating agencies frequently set aside, or are willing to set aside, part of their budget for research purposes. The resources of these agencies, particularly the federal agencies, have been reviewed (Williams, 1963).

There is no doubt that the researcher's experience in relating to granting agencies has much to do with his success in obtaining financial support for his work. Indeed, his experience may include not only his own attempts to secure support for his work, but also his activities and energies on the other side of the table, as a member of panels responsible for advising on and approving research support for others.

DIFFERENCES IN GRANTSMANSHIP

The novice applying for a grant may become discouraged as he seems to find that certain people are more successful in obtaining funds than others. At times, one hears comments about favoritism or about having to be a member of the establishment, as explanations of the rejection of one research plan in the face of the acceptance and support of another. Undoubtedly, there is a certain amount of professional colleagueship among researchers and persons in funding agencies, and it does influence who receives what. Certainly it is fair to say that those in a position to recommend or disapprove support, including the peers of the researcher who are members of study sections and councils of various funding agencies, take into account their personal estimate of the man. In almost all research, one bets on the investigator as well as the importance of the problem or the elegance of the design. However, most of the inequities that occur are probably related to the investigator's skill in writing up and selling the study, as well as to differences in cost, the relative scientific worth of the study, and the relevance and importance to social policy of the problem. The social-policy researcher needs colleagues and critics whose experience and wisdom stem from having worked with a fair degree of success in the area which interests him.

Obviously, the social-policy researcher must understand something of the workings of the various research-supporting agencies, particularly the ones to which he is most likely to relate. There are considerable differences, for example, within the U.S. Public Health Services—between the various National Institutes of Health and the more action and practice-oriented bureaus. And the Public Health Service certainly differs from other bodies within the Department of Health, Education, and Welfare which provide grant support. And so on; there are other Federal departments as well as local, state, and private funding groups. A failure to recognize the differences and to be sensitive to the interests of the parties and processes involved in obtaining support may be highly detrimental to the researcher's work.

THE LURE OF FUNDS

As we have just seen, the social-policy researcher must pay real attention to financial support if he is to accomplish his work. On the other hand, he must avoid becoming too involved in fund raising or too responsive to pressure to orient his work to the marketplace. From time to time, different social areas are given high priority. Sometimes this is a consequence of political activity and the reaction of policy makers to pressure from their constituents; at other times it is primarily an attempt to stimulate more work in a neglected but important field.

Academicians and researchers also promote and emphasize different fields at different points. While it is probably true that the isolated expressions of social critics or social scientists do not in themselves shift things markedly, one is still quite aware that such volumes as Michael Harrington's (1963) study of poverty, William White's *The Organization Man* (1956) and Moynihan's (1965) study of black families have had an important impact on research and on its support.

The social-policy researcher, thus, has several loyalties to juggle. The first, and perhaps the most important, is his loyalty to those matters about which he has specialized knowledge and in which he has some career interests. A second is toward the policy-makers' view of what social problems are most important. The third is toward the consistency of his work with the mainstream of academic thought at a particular point in time. All these considerations impinge upon the matter of financial support. In general, however, sound work will be supported by one means or another. With a minimum of compromise, the social-policy researcher should be able to secure adequate funds for his work and keep the policy makers happy. A measure of independence and autonomy must remain an integral part of his role.

INTERPERSONAL SUPPORT

There is another kind of support, however, which is crucial, the respect and recognition of colleagues as well as policy makers. Often, the types of research that social-policy researchers engage in are considered avant-garde or radical, but sometimes the research is seen as conservative, and supporting the *status quo*. The problem does not become visible and public very often but, when it does, it creates considerable discomfort. One illustration is Project Camelot (Horowitz, 1967), a study, of the processes of social change in a Latin-American country supported by the Department of Defense and undertaken by American University. Admittedly, a number of inadvisable choices were made by the research team as it developed relationships in the community and planned the project, errors which irritated a number of important people in the country under study. The project was also caught up in the squabbles of the Department of Defense and the Department of State about who should be sponsoring such research. When the project received adverse publicity, the fact of its sponsorship by the Department of Defense led a number of social scientists to view it as a research endeavor directed at maintaining the *status quo*. Rather than rallying to the support of the research team, who in retrospect have been judged by many to have been innocent of the charges against them, though perhaps naïve, the academic community was mostly unsympathetic and nonsupportive.

The obvious conclusion is that investigators undertaking social-policy research are well advised to keep open their channels of communication with their peers and to be alert to the possibility that certain kinds of sponsorship may involve them in serious political squabbles.

Ethical Standards

Ethical standards and guidelines for social-policy researchers have not been sufficiently developed. One important issue revolves around the confidentiality of research findings. Sometimes, making research findings public might do irreparable harm to the sponsor or community. Like many other issues discussed in this volume, there are no clear-cut rules to set forth. One must hope that the humanitarianism of the investigators is above reproach and that they can be depended upon to recognize their responsibilities to their colleagues and to the general community.

From time to time, social-policy researchers are subjected to unscrupulous demands. For example, at a meeting of public-opinion researchers, discussing some political polling that took place during the Kennedy-Nixon election, the question came up of the right of the sponsor of the poll, in this case a Kennedy campaign group, to release only part of the findings. The general view at this meeting, and the general position held by statesmen in the field of survey research, is that the sponsor is obligated to provide a consistent policy: either the surveys should be made public in their entirety or they should not be released at all. It is argued that the partial release of information may result in an unfair advantage to one candidate. A somewhat different but related stand is taken by several nonprofit survey research groups, who insist that if the researchers themselves do not make reports of their work available after a given period of time, they have the option and right to do so. Beyond a few basic guidelines, however, the research world operates without clear policies, and social control is highly informal.

PRIVACY

The issue of privacy, as noted before, which is related to the problem of the confidentiality of findings, has become more important in the recent past. In part, the problem has emerged because the design of some studies has required the investigator to be deceptive about the reasons for his research. To give an informant false reasons for gathering information from him is regarded as highly unethical by some investigators. There are other invasion-of-privacy issues as well. For example, in order to ascertain who in the community was in a particular income bracket, a research group obtained the cooperation of the community's credit bureau and was given access to credit reports, without the permission of the persons studied.

There are no hard-and-fast rules about what is unethical practice, but clearly, deception or the use of privileged information without the permission of the persons involved should be employed sparingly. It is defensible only when the problem is of utmost importance and it is impossible to conduct the research in other ways (Ruebhausen and Brim, 1965). But while gross violations of privacy may and should be rare, the matter is coming increasingly to public attention. For example, at Congressional hearings held on the development of a national program of indicators of social conditions, one of the chief concerns of the Committee was the possibility of the invasion of privacy (U.S. Congress, 1969). In the long run, it is doubtful that the simple assurances of respected social scientists are going to prove sufficient to allay the public's fears; its concern with the possible invasion of privacy, like that with the confidentiality of research results, undoubtedly will intensify.

Concluding Comment

In this final chapter, we have described some aspects of the day-to-day work of the social-policy researcher. There is much that needs to be codified and specified about how social-policy research is undertaken. At the outset of the volume, we discussed the importance of the posture of the social-policy researchers in distinguishing him from his peers in other social-science research. The social scientist who desires to undertake policy studies, to be an agent of social change and contribute constructively to the solution and amelioration of the myriad of problems in today's communities must recognize that more than technical knowledge and craftsmanship is involved. The way he conducts himself, the types of interpersonal relationships he develops, and the attention he pays to various administrative and organizational tasks are equally crucial to the successful fulfillment of his role.

It should be possible, at some future date, to describe the dynamics of policy research more specifically and fully. We anticipate further growth in the quality and quantity of social-policy research and increased consideration of how the day-to-day work is undertaken. We can visualize an increased structuring of the role of the social-policy researcher and a greater institutionalization of the settings in which work is accomplished —perhaps the social-problem research institutes recommended by Brim and his committee of the National Academy of Sciences—National Science Board (National Science Foundation, 1969). Such developments, along with the continued interest of policy makers in the social-research enterprise, will make it easier for the research worker to contribute to the solutions of the problems of our communities.

SELECTED REFERENCES

ADORNO, T. W., *et al.*
  1950   *The Authoritarian Personality.* New York: Harper & Row, Publishers, Inc.

AMERICAN HOSPITAL ASSOCIATION
  1962   to present *Blue Cross Reports.*

ANDREWS, FRANK M.
  1964   "Scientific research as related to teaching or administration." *Administrative Science Quarterly* 9 (September): 182–93.

ANGELL, ROBERT C.
  1967   "The ethical problems of applied sociology," in Paul F. Lazarsfeld and William Wilensky (eds.), The Uses of Sociology. New York: Basic Books, Inc., Publishers.

BAHN, ANITA, *et al.*
  1961   "Diagnostic and demographic characteristics of patients seen in outpatient psychiatric clinic for an entire state (Maryland)." *American Journal of Psychiatry* 117 (March): 798–801.

BARBER, BERNARD, AND RENÉE C. FOX
  1959   "The case of the floppy-eared rabbits: An instance of seren-

dipity gained and serendipity lost." *The American Journal of Sociology* 64 (September): 128–36.

BAUER, RAYMOND A. (ed.)
1966 *Social Indicators: A First Approximation.* Cambridge, Mass.: The MIT Press.

BAUER, RAYMOND, AND KENNETH J. GERGEN (eds.)
1968 *The Study of Policy Formation.* New York: The Free Press.

BECKER, HOWARD S.
1955 "Marihuana use and social control." *Social Problems* 3 (July): 35–44.

————, *et al.*
1961 *Boys in White.* Chicago: University of Chicago Press.

————
1966 *Social Problems: A Modern Approach.* New York: John Wiley & Sons, Inc.

BENNIS, WARREN S.
1963 "A new role for the behavioral sciences: Effecting organizational change." *Administrative Science Quarterly* 8 (September): 125–63.

BERNAL, J. D.
1967 *The Social Function of Science.* Cambridge, Mass.: The MIT Press.

BIDERMAN, A.
1968 "Dollars and scholars." Mimeographed.

BLALOCK, HUBERT M., JR.
1964 *Causal Inferences in Non-experimental Research.* Chapel Hill: University of North Carolina Press.

BORGATTA, EDGAR F.
1959 "The new principle of psychotherapy." *Journal of Clinical Psychology* 15 (July): 330–34.

BRAYFIELD, ARTHUR H.
1967 "Psychology and public affairs." *American Psychologist* 22 (March): 182–86.

BRUNNER, EDMUND
1962 "Social research dollars and sense." *Public Opinion Quarterly* 2 (Spring): 97–101.

BRUYN, SEVERYN
1966 *Human Perspective in Sociology.* Englewood Cliffs, N.J.: Prentice-Hall, Inc.

CAREY, ALEX
1967 "The Hawthorne Studies: A radical criticism." *American Sociological Review* 32 (June): 403–16.

CAUDILL, WILLIAM A.
　1958　*The Psychiatric Hospital as a Small Society.* Cambridge, Mass.: Harvard University Press.

CLARK, KENNETH B.
　1955　"Desegregation in the Public Schools." *Social Problems* 2 (April): entire volume.

CLINE, HUGH F., *et al.*
　1968　"The Analysis and evaluation of detached-worker programs," in Stanton Wheeler (ed.), *Controlling Delinquents,* pp. 287–315. New York: John Wiley & Sons, Inc.

CLOWARD, RICHARD A., AND LLOYD E. OHLIN
　1960　*Delinquency and Opportunity: A Theory of Delinquent Gangs.* New York: The Free Press.

COCHRAN, W. G., AND G. COX
　1950　*Experimental Designs.* New York: John Wiley & Sons, Inc.

COHEN, JACOB
　1968　"Multiple regression as a general data-analytic system." *Psychological Bulletin* 65 (November): 426–43.

COSTNER, HERBERT L., AND ROBERT K. LEIK
　1964　"Deductions from axiomatic theory." *American Sociological Review* 29 (December): 819–35.

COTTRELL, LEONARD S., JR., AND ELEANOR BERNERT SHELDON
　1963　"Problems of collaboration between social scientists and the practicing professions." *Annals* 346 (March): 126–37.

COUCH, A., AND K. KENISTON
　1960　"Yeasayers and naysayers: Agreeing response set as a personality variable." *Journal of Abnormal and Social Psychiatry.* 60 (March): 151–74.

DOHRENWEND, BARBARA S., *et al.*
　1968　"Social resistance and interviewer effects." *Public Opinion Quarterly* 52 (Fall): 410–22.

DUFF, RAYMOND S., *et al.*
　1968　*Sickness and Society.* New York: Harper & Row Publishers, Inc.

DUGGAN, THOMAS J., AND CHARLES W. DEAN
　1968　"Common misinterpretations of significance levels in sociological journals." *The American Sociologist* 3 (February): 45–46.

DUNCAN, OTIS DUDLEY
　1966　"Path analysis: Sociological examples." *American Journal of Sociology* 72 (July): 1–16.

———, *et al.*
  1968   "Peer influences on aspirations: A reinterpretation." *American Journal of Sociology* 74 (September): 119–37.

EDWARDS, ALLEN L.
  1957   *The Social Desirability Variable in Personality Assessment and Research.* New York: Dryden Press, Inc.

———
  1967   *Experimental Design in Psychological Research.* New York: Holt, Rinehart & Winston, Inc.

ELINSON, JACK
  1963   "Methods of sociomedical research," in Howard E. Freeman, Sol Levine, and Leo G. Reader (eds.), *Handbook of Medical Sociology,* pp. 449–72. Englewood Cliffs, N.J.: Prentice-Hall, Inc.

EMPEY, LAMAR, AND JEROME RABOW
  1961   "The Provo experiment in delinquency rehabilitation." *American Sociological Review* 26 (October): 679–95.

EZEKIEL, MORDECAI, AND KARL A. FOX
  1959   *Methods of Correlation and Regression.* New York: John Wiley & Sons, Inc.

FESTINGER, LEON
  1964   "Behavioral support for opinion changes." *Public Opinion Quarterly* 28 (Fall): 404–17.

FOX, RENÉE
  1959   *Experiment Perilous: Physicians and Patients Facing the Unknown.* New York: The Free Press.

FREEMAN, HOWARD E., AND H. ASHLEY WEEKS
  1956   "Analysis of a program of treatment of delinquent boys." *American Journal of Sociology* 42 (July): 56–61.

———, AND OZZIE G. SIMMONS
  1960   "The use of the survey in mental illness research." *Mental Hygiene* 44 (July): 400–410.

———, AND CLARENCE C. SHERWOOD
  1965   "Research in large-scale intervention programs." *The Journal of Social Issues* 21 (January): 11–28.

———, AND JOHN F. SCOTT
  1966   "A critical review of alcohol education for adolescents." *Community Mental Health Journal* 2 (Fall): 222–30.

GEER, BLANCHE
  1964   "First days in the field," in Phillip E. Hammond (ed.),

Sociologists at Work: Essays on the Craft of Social Research,
pp. 332–44. New York: Basic Books, Inc., Publishers.

——, *et al.*
1968   "Learning the ropes: Situational learning in four occupa-
        tional training programs," in Irwin Deutscher and Elizabeth
        Thompson (eds.), *Among the People: Studies of the Urban
        Poor,* pp. 209–33. New York: Basic Books, Inc., Publishers.
        [See also: Stephen J. Miller, 1966, "Exchange of negotiated
        learning." *Sociological Quarterly* 7 (Autumn): 469–79.]

GIBBS, JACK P.
1966   "Suicide," in Robert K. Merton and Robert A. Nisbet (eds.),
        Contemporary Social Problems. New York: Harcourt, Brace
        & World, Inc.

GIL, DAVID G.
1969   "Incidence of child abuse and demographic characteristics,"
        in Ray E. Helfer and C. Henry Kempe (eds.), *The Battered
        Child,* pp. 19–40. Chicago: University of Chicago Press.

GOLD, DAVID
1969   "Statistical tests and substantive significance." *The American
        Sociologist* 4 (February): 42–46.

GOODMAN, LEO A.
1965   "On the multivariate analysis of three dichotomous vari-
        ables," *American Journal of Sociology* 71 (November): 290–
        301.

GOULDNER, ALVIN
1962   "Anti-minotaur: The myth of a value-free sociology." *Social
        Problems* 9 (Winter): 199–213.

GROSS, BERTRAM M., (ed.)
1967   "Social goals and indicators for American society." *Annals of
        the American Academy of Political and Social Science* 2
        (September): entire volume.

HABENSTEIN, ROBERT W., AND HOWARD S. BECKER
1969   *Field Methods.* Chicago: Aldine Press.

HAMMOND, PHILIP E., (ed.)
1964   *Sociologist at Work.* New York: Basic Books, Inc., Publishers.

HARRINGTON, MICHAEL
1963   *The Other America: Poverty in the United States.* New York:
        The Macmillan Company.

HERRING, PENDLETON
1965   "Political science in the next decade." *American Political
        Science Review* 59 (August): 757–66.

HOLLINGSHEAD, A. B., AND F. C. REDLICH
1958 *Social Class and Mental Illness.* New York: John Wiley & Sons, Inc.

HOMANS, GEORGE C.
1950 *The Human Group.* New York: Harcourt, Brace & World, Inc.

HOROWITZ, IRVING L., (ed.)
1967 "Studies in the relationship between social sciences and practical politics," in *Rise and Fall of Project Camelot.* Cambridge, Mass.: The MIT Press.

HORST, PAUL
1941 *The Prediction of Personal Adjustment.* New York: Social Science Research Council.

HOVLAND, C. I., *et al.*
1949 *Experiments in Mass Communication.* Studies in Social Psychology in World War II, Vol. 3. Princeton, N.J.: Princeton University Press.

HOWTON, F. WILLIAM
1963 "Work assignment and interpersonal relations in a research organization." *Administrative Science Quarterly* 7 (March): 502–20.

HYMAN, H. H.
1955 *Survey Design and Analysis: Principles, Cases and Procedures.* New York: The Free Press.

JONES, KENNETH J.
forth-
coming
"Multi-predictor analysis of variance and covariance for one-way and multiple-way designs," in *Multi-Variate Methodology.* New York: McGraw-Hill Book Company.

KAHN, ALFRED J.
1969 *Theory and Practice of Social Planning.* New York: Russell Sage Foundation.

KANTOR, DAVID, AND WILLIAM IRA BENNETT
1968 "Orientations of street-corner workers and their effect on gangs," in Stanton Wheeler (ed.), *Controlling Delinquents,* pp. 271–86. New York: John Wiley & Sons, Inc.

KAPLAN, NORMAN
1959 "The role of the research administrator." *Administrative Science Quarterly* 9 (June): 20–42.

KELMAN, HERBERT C.

1965   "The social consequences of social research: A new social issue." *Journal of Social Issues* 21 (January): 21–40.

――――

1968   *A Time to Speak: On Human Values and Social Research.* San Francisco: Jossey-Bass.

KINSEY, A. C., *et al.*
1948   *Sexual Behavior in the Human Male.* Philadelphia: W. B. Saunders Co.

KISH, LESLIE
1965   *Survey Sampling.* New York: John Wiley & Sons, Inc.

KLERMAN, GERALD L.
1966   "The social milieu and drug response in psychiatric patients." Paper presented at the American Sociological Association, Miami.

LAMBERT, CAMILLE, AND HOWARD E. FREEMAN
1967   *The Clinic Habit.* New Haven, Conn.: College and Universities Press.

LAZARSFELD, PAUL F., *et al.*
1948   *People's Choice.* New York: Columbia University Press.

――――, *et al.*
1967   *The Uses of Sociology.* New York: Basic Books, Inc., Publishers.

――――, AND MORRIS ROSENBERG
1955   *The Language of Social Research.* New York: The Free Press.

LECHT, LEONARD A.
1966   *Goals, Priorities, and Dollars: The Next Decade.* New York: The Free Press.

LEMBERG CENTER FOR THE STUDY OF VIOLENCE
1967   *Six-City Study: A Survey of Racial Attitudes in Six Northern Cities: Preliminary Findings.* Waltham, Mass.: Brandeis University.

LENSKI, GERHARD E.
1954   "Status crystallization: A nonvertical dimension of social status." *American Sociological Review* 19 (August): 405–13.

LERNER, DANIEL
1959   "Social science: Whence and whither?" in Daniel Lerner (ed.), *The Human Meaning of the Social Sciences,* pp. 13–35. Cleveland: World Publishing Company.

LINDQUIST, E. F.
1956 *Design and Analysis of Experiments in Psychology and Education.* Boston: Houghton Mifflin Company.

LOOMIS, CHARLES P.
1960 *Social Systems: Essays on their Persistence and Change.* Princeton, N.J.: D. Van Nostrand Co., Inc.

MACMAHON, BRIAN, *et al.*
1960 *Epidemiologic Methods.* Boston: Little, Brown and Company.

MADGE, JOHN
1962 *The Origins of Scientific Sociology.* New York: The Free Press.

MARROW, ALFRED J.
1964 "Risks and uncertainties in action research." *Journal of Social Issues* 20 (July): 5–20.

MERTON, ROBERT K., AND ALICE KITTS
1950 (Robert K. Merton and Paul F. Lazarsfeld, eds.), *Continuities in Social Research.* New York: The Free Press.

MERTON, ROBERT K., AND ROBERT A. NISBET (eds.)
1966 *Contemporary Social Problems* (2nd ed.). New York: Harcourt, Brace & World, Inc.

MILLER, D. C.
1964 *Handbook of Research Design and Social Measurement.* New York: David McKay Co., Inc.

MILLER, STEPHEN J., AND W. D. BRYANT
1964 *A Division of Nursing Labor.* Kansas City, Mo.: Community Studies, Inc.

MILLER, S. M., AND FRANK RIESSMAN
1968 *Social Class and Social Policy.* New York: Basic Books, Inc., Publishers.

MILLIKAN, MAX F.
1959 "The relation of knowledge to action," in Daniel Lerner (ed.), *The Human Meaning of the Social Sciences,* pp. 158–82. Cleveland: World Publishing Company.

MONDALE, WALTER F.
1968 Statement on the use of social indicators for policy purposes. *S. 843, Subcommittee on Government Research of the Committee on Government Operations of the U.S. Senate.* Part 2. Washington, D.C.: Government Printing Office.

MOORE, WILBERT E., AND ELEANOR B. SHELDON
   1968   *The Measurement of Social Change*. New York: Russell Sage
           Foundation.

MORRIS, ROBERT, AND ROBERT H. BINSTOCK
   1966   "Decisions confronting a planning specialist." *Social Service
           Review* 40 (March): 8–14.

MOYNIHAN, DANIEL P.
   1965   *The Negro Family*. Office of Policy Planning and Research
           (March). Washington, D.C.: United States Department of
           Labor.

NATIONAL ACADEMY OF SCIENCES
   1969   *The Behavioral and Social Sciences*. Washington, D.C.: Na-
           tional Academy of Science.

NATIONAL SCIENCE FOUNDATION
   1969   *Knowledge Into Action: Improving the Nation's Use of the
           Social Sciences*. Washington, D.C.: U.S. Government Printing
           Office.

NYE, F. IVAN, AND JAMES F. SHORT, JR.
   1957   "Scaling delinquent behavior." *American Sociological Re-
           view* 22 (June): 326–31.

ODUM, HOWARD W.
   1951   *American Sociology*. (A Study of Sociology in the United
           States through 1950). New York: Longmans, Green & Co.,
           Inc.

PETERSON, OSLER L., *et al.*
   1956   "An analytical study of North Carolina general practice:
           1953–1954." *Journal of Medical Education* 31 (December)
           Part 2.

PRESIDENT'S COMMISSION ON LAW ENFORCEMENT AND ADMINISTRATION OF
JUSTICE
   1967   *The Challenge of Crime in a Free Society*. Washington, D.C.:
           U.S. Government Printing Office.

_____
   1967   "The administration of juvenile justice: The juvenile court
           and related methods of delinquency control." *Task Force
           Report: Juvenile Delinquency and Youth Crime,* pp. 1–40.
           Washington, D.C.: U.S. Government Printing Office.

_____
   1967   "The amount and trends of crime." *Task Force Report:
           Crime and Its Impact—An Assessment,* pp. 14–40. Washing-
           ton, D.C.: U.S. Government Printing Office.

RANNEY, AUSTIN
1968 "The study of policy content: A framework for choice."
Items 22 (September): 25–31.

————, (ed.)
1968 *Political Science and Public Policy*. Chicago: Markham Publishing Company.

RICHARDSON, STEPHEN A., *et al.*
1965 *Interviewing*. New York: Basic Books, Inc., Publishers.

ROBINS, LEE N.
1966 *Deviant Children Grown Up*. Baltimore: Williams & Wilkins Co.

ROETHLISBERGER, F. J., AND WILLIAM J. DICKSON
1939 *Management and the Worker*. Cambridge, Mass.: Harvard University Press.

ROSENTHAL, ROBERT, AND LENORE JACOBSON
1968 *Pygmalion in the Classroom: Teacher Expectation and Pupils' Intellectual Development*. New York: Holt, Rinehart & Winston, Inc.

ROTHWELL, CHARLES E.
1951 "Foreword," in Daniel Lerner and Harold D. Lasswell (eds.), *The Policy Sciences*. Cambridge, Mass.: The MIT Press.

RUEBHAUSEN, OSCAR M., AND ORVILLE G. BRIM, JR.
1965 "Privacy and behavioral research." *Columbia Law Review* 65 (November): 1184–1211.

SAWYER, JACK AND HOWARD SCHECHTER
1968 "Computers, privacy and the national data center: The responsibility of social scientists." *American Psychologist* 23 (November): 810–17.

SELLIN, THORSTEN, AND MARVIN E. WOLFGANG
1964 *The Measurement of Delinquency*. New York: John Wiley & Sons, Inc.

SEWELL, WILLIAM H., AND J. MICHAEL ARMER
1966 "Neighborhood context and college plans." *American Sociological Review* 31 (April): 159–68.

SIMMONS, OZZIE G.
1967 *Work and Mental Illness*. New York: John Wiley & Sons, Inc.

SKOLNICK, JEROME H.
1966 *Justice without Trial: Law Enforcement in Democratic Society*. New York: John Wiley & Sons, Inc.

SMIGEL, ERWIN O.
    1964   The Wall Street Lawyer: Professional Organization Man?
            New York: The Free Press.
STANTON, ALFRED, AND MORRIS SCHWARTZ
    1954   The Mental Hospital. New York: Basic Books, Inc., Pub-
            lishers.
STOUFFER, S. A., et al.
    1949   Studies in Social Psychology in World War II, The American
            Soldier: Adjustment During Army Life. Vol. 1. Princeton,
            N.J.: Princeton University Press.

    1949   The American Soldier: And Its Aftermath. Ibid., Vol. II.

    1949   Experiments in Mass Communication. Ibid., Vol. III.

    1950   Measurement and Prediction. Ibid., Vol. IV.
STRAUS, R.
    1957   "The nature and status of medical sociology." American
            Sociological Review 22 (April): 200–204.
SUCHMAN, EDWARD A.
    1967   Evaluative Research: Principles and Practice in Public Ser-
            vice and Social Action Programs. New York: Russell Sage
            Foundation.
ULLMAN, L.
    1967   Institution and Outcome: A Comparative Study of Psychi-
            atric Hospitals. New York: Pergamon Press.
U.S. CONGRESS, SENATE
    1969   Congressional Record, 91st Congress 115, 9 (January): 1.
U.S. CONGRESS, SENATE SUBCOMMITTEE ON GOVERNMENT RESEARCH
    1968   Hearing on S. 843.
U.S. DEPARTMENT OF COMMERCE
    1969   Statistical Abstract of the United States. Washington, D.C.:
            Government Printing Office.
U.S. DEPARTMENT OF HEALTH, EDUCATION, AND WELFARE
    1966   Medical Subject Headings, Vol. 7, No. 1, Part 2 (January).
            Washington, D.C.: Government Printing Office.
U.S. DEPARTMENT OF HEALTH, EDUCATION, AND WELFARE
    1968   Planning, Program and Budgeting. Washington, D.C.: Gov-
            ernment Printing Office.
WALD, PATRICIA M.
    1967   "Poverty and criminal justice," in President's Commission on

Law Enforcement and Administration of Justice, *Task Force Report: The Courts,* pp. 139–51. Washington, D.C.: Government Printing Office.

WALTON, JOHN
1966 "Discipline, method, and community power: A note on the sociology of knowledge." *American Sociological Review* 31 (October): 684–89.

WARREN, ROLAND L.
1969 "Model cities first round: Politics, planning, and participation," in *Journal of the American Institute of Planners,* 35 (July): 245–52.

WEISS, CAROL H.
1968 *Validity of Interview Responses of Welfare Mothers.* New York: Bureau of Applied Social Research, Columbia University.

WHYTE, WILLIAM FOOTE
1955 *Street Corner Society.* Chicago: The University of Chicago Press.

WHYTE, WILLIAM H.
1956 *The Organization Man.* New York: Simon & Schuster, Inc.

WILDAVSKY, AARON
1967 "The political economy of efficiency." *The Public Interest* 8 (Summer): 30–48.

WILKINS, LESLIE T.
1969 *Evaluation of Penal Measures.* New York: Random House, Inc.

WILLIAMS, RICHARD H.
1963 "The strategy of sociomedical research," in Howard E. Freeman, Sol Levine, and Leo G. Reeder (eds.), *Handbook of Medical Sociology,* pp. 423–48. Englewood Cliffs, N.J.: Prentice-Hall, Inc.

WILLIAMS, ROBIN MURPHY
1951 *American Society: A Sociological Interpretation.* New York: Alfred A. Knopf, Inc.

WILNER, D. M., *et al.*
1962 *The Housing Environment and Family Life.* Baltimore: The John Hopkins University Press.

WILSON, JAMES Q.
1968 "The police and the delinquent in two cities," in S. Wheeler (ed.), *Controlling Delinquents,* pp. 9–30. New York: John Wiley & Sons, Inc.

WOOD, BRYCE AND MANUEL DIÉGUES, JR. (eds.)
    1967   "Social science in Latin America: March 29–31, 1965. *Items*
            21 (June): 13–17.
ZELDITCH, MORRIS, JR.
    1962   "Some methodological problems of field studies." *American
            Journal of Sociology* 68 (March): 566–76.

INDEX